FORM AND LINE

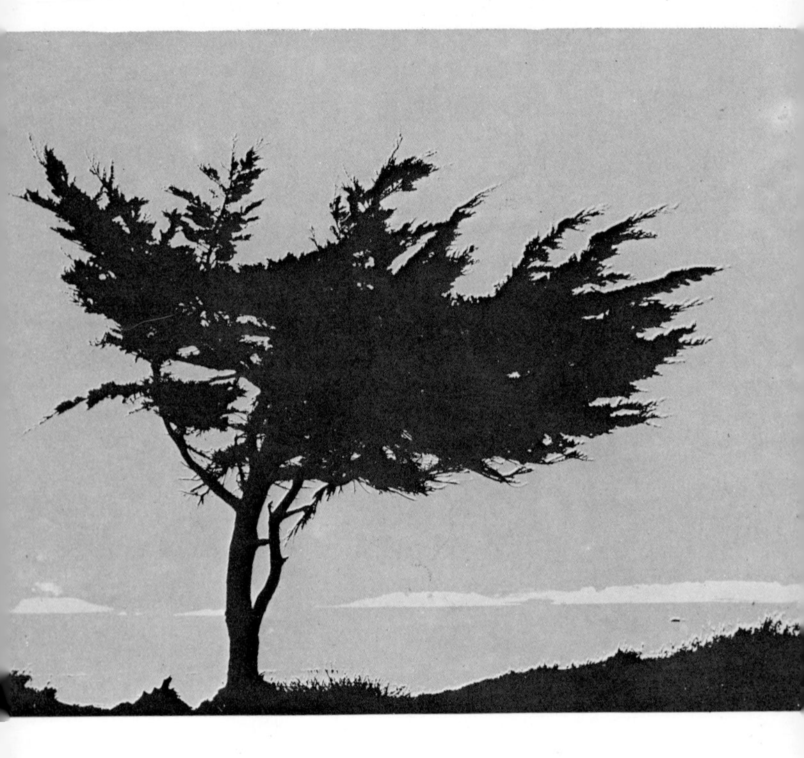

An introduction to photographic design and derivatives

By
Hans Götze

Translated by Mike Shields
for Cave Translations Ltd, London
Edited by R. H. Mason FIIP, Hon FRPS.

Argus Books Ltd,
14 St James Road,
Watford,
Herts,
England.

First Published 1980

ISBN 0 85242 703 4

Printed and bound by G. A. Pindar & Son Limited, Scarborough, England

Contents

All photographs in this book, are by the author.

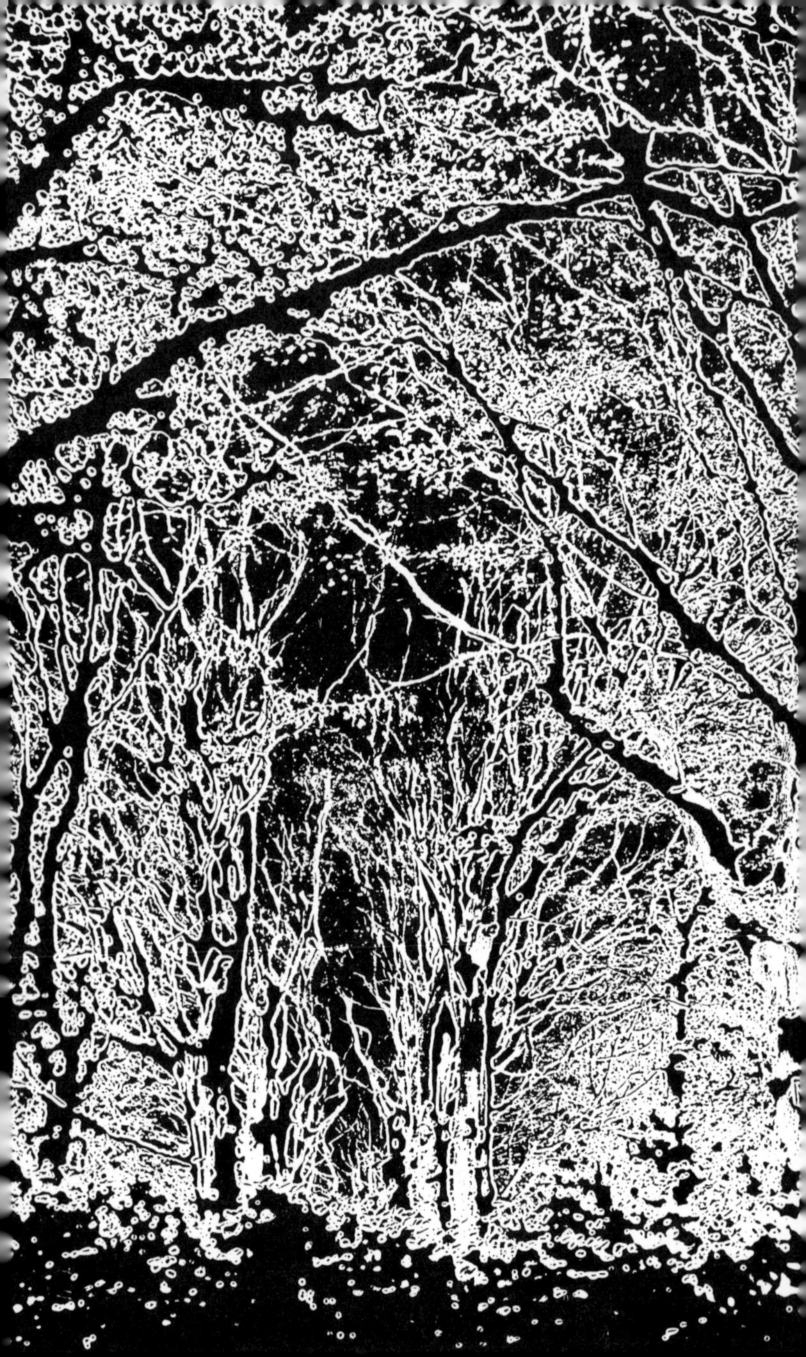

1. Introduction

For years now, argument has raged as to whether or not photography is art. One result of this, it seems, is the trend to define it as having a "place of its own", and the protagonists of this "place" – a safe place, but a little isolated – are usually photographers who have been pushed out of the "art-or-not-art" discussions which take place in every club. Now it is undoubtedly best to walk away from such discussions with a shrug and I wouldn't even bring it up here were it not for the way in which these photographic isolationists keep on coining phrases like "typically photographic" or "pure photography". In this way, a tiny minority is likely to spoil the pleasure of the rest of us with its dogmatic mentality.

You can see the sort of thing these people get up to at the exhibitions they organize. They are full of taboos and definitions of what photography is or is not, what it is eminently fit for, and what is unsuitable for it.

But the facts are that the possibilities of photographic techniques are so great that they couldn't be fully documented in a whole lifetime. Photography has far more to it than just grabbing the graphic subject before it vanishes.

At a period of time when virtually nothing is "pure", where painters use plaster and press-cuttings in their paintings, and where all rules are broken as a matter of course, it seems a little ridiculous to insist that photography alone should remain pure and stick firmly in the rut of its own traditions. Surely it can't be expected to go on forever producing nice little snapshots of Auntie Lizzie in black-and-white?

The fact is, of course, that photographic technique is considerably more versatile than this and it is by making use of this versatility that personal characteristics and tastes can be brought into the area of photographic work.

Of course, if you do this sort of thing, you may possibly expose yourself to mockery. It was fairly recently that a well-known critic scornfully dismissed this sort of work as "darkroom athletics", while at the same time, and in the very same column, writing enthusiastically on the fascinating potential of screen printing which is, needless to say, a purely (if you'll pardon the expression) photographic process.

The main trouble seems to lie with the idea that something artistic can come out of such a cold and technical machine as a camera. It is as if there has been some cunning publicity campaign selling the opinion that, in art, anything worth having must of necessity be difficult. It doesn't seem to occur to the proponents of these ideas that it can be possible, through the intelligent and careful use of technical processes, to achieve artistic results which represent the emotions of the person producing them.

And this is indeed where the art and science of photographic derivations lies: in the making of images that more accurately represent the feelings and emotions of the photographer. It is a way of getting more expression into photography.

But you can take as many photographs as you like of flowers, windmills and girls (with or without bikinis), and even be regarded as something of a portrait painter. You can make money at it sometimes. But start on derivations and you're into something entirely different. Just try it, and you'll know by the meagre applause your works get at the next club night that you have just managed to label yourself as yet another superficial technician!

This is something you just have to get used to if you want to go ahead with derivations, even though photography is a much more difficult medium to work with than, say, drawing, if you want to get feeling and emotion into your work. Otto Croy has asked the question – is it better to use an internal combustion engine with which to drive along the road or to fly? It's a good question but in some ways a little irrelevent. It is like the question we started out with, about whether or not photography is an art. The answer to that one, at least, is that it depends on how much of an artist the photographer is himself.

Photographic derivations is a term that covers a number of graphic techniques. It includes, for example, double image prints which don't have any graphic content at all, strictly speaking. However, in this book, we shall assume that derivatives covers all methods that can be used on a negative to give a more subjective interpretation of the subject.

Photographic derivations are frequently confused with experimental photography. What often happens is that the photographer presents his work, somewhat sheepishly perhaps, as an experiment so that he can retire behind the "work-in-progress" excuse when he runs into adverse criticism. But an experiment, clearly, is an exercise the outcome of which is an unknown quantity. If you know what the result is going to be, then what you are doing can't be an experiment.

Experiments are all very well in the laboratory where you can try out new things to your heart's content without being at all sure whether the final product will be miracle or a disaster. But I can tell you here and now that the techniques of derivatives are well established. If you use a given technique in the right way, the results will be completely predictable.

And here we come to the essential heart of photographic derivation. In ordinary photography you start with an object and work towards a

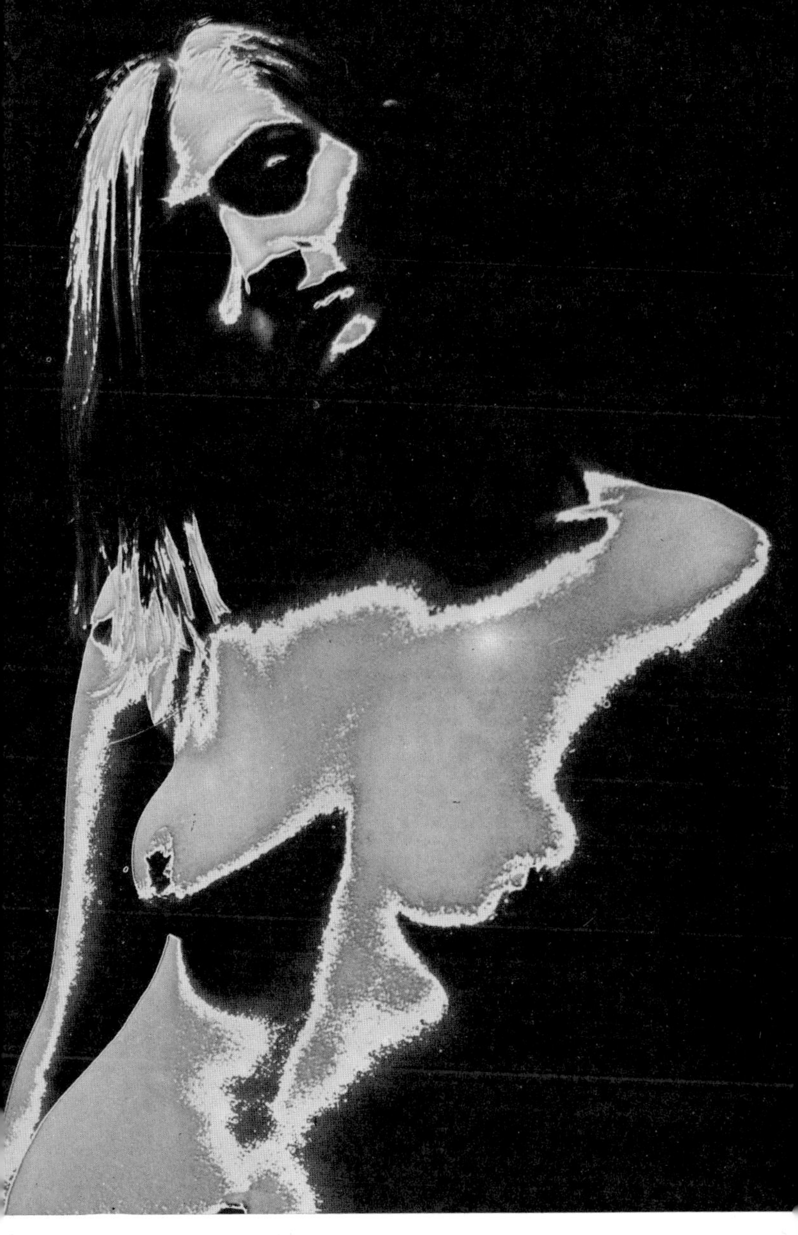

final result. With derivatives the opposite is the case. You start with a final result in mind and choose the objects and techniques which will produce that result for you.

As you can see, then, the ability to imagine , or envisage this final result is an essential to the art of derivation. The photographer must be able to see a picture in his mind's eye and then work backwards from that picture, through the techniques that will be used to produce it to the sort of object which will be needed to start the process off.

This implies that you can't just start off with some arbitrary negative and end up with something wonderful. There is no technique in existence that will make a good photograph out of a bad one. But it is always possible to make a good negative better by concentrating on the attractive aspects and toning down its weaknesses.

Photographic derivation is an area that can produce a lot of disappointment. If the result you produce is not the result that you originally envisaged then, it has to be regarded as a failure no matter how pretty it may look. One the other hand, the satisfaction gained when you do achieve what you were trying for has to be experienced to be believed.

The techniques that I give you in this book will not always be easy. In some cases, they are difficult – but never overpoweringly so. As long as you work carefully and accurately, you will find they will come out the way you want them to.

Previsualization

By previsualization, we mean that exercise of the imagination on the part of the photographer whereby he forms in his mind a clear impression of the desired result before actually taking the photograph.

It doesn't matter whether you are taking a simple landscape or making some complex multiple-image photogram. You still have to ask yourself the same question – how is this going to look when I come to print it? More to the point – what have I got to do to get that effect? How can I capture the essence of this subject? What combination of exposure, filters, aperture, developer and print will be needed to give the result I have in mind? At the same time, we must be careful not to fool ourselves. While a record of a particular time or event can certainly recall an emotion, it is by no means a record of the emotion itself.

However, on the pages that follow you will learn how to add that essential dimension of emotion to what would otherwise be just a record.

Another point I want to stress before we get into technicalities is that I am making no claim for completeness. There are many more possibilities than I can cram into this little book. What I hope will happen is that the ideas I give you here will take root and produce further ideas in your mind; that they will, as it were, act as a catalyst for your imagination.

And it is imagination – imagination and memory – that are the main qualities needed, especially at the previsualization stage. You need memory because you must be able to recall exactly what you already have on file that can be used to improve or fill out a given subject. You need imagination to be able to envisage the possibilities presented by a given subject, so that you can choose which one to use.

Most people have these qualities and they can be brought out by study training. You may make a few blunders at first but that doesn't matter so long as you learn from them. For, in derivation as in anything else, you can learn only by experience.

2. Photography without a camera

Photograms

Put a piece of photographic paper under the enlarger. Choose a few transparent or semi-transparent objects and place one or more of them on the paper. Expose with a white light (short exposure for grey background, long for black background) and develop the paper in the usual way. The result will be a white "shadow" of the subject on a black or grey-toned background. Depending on the choice of subject, you will produce strictly literal or artistically abstract photographs.

With a little forethought and imagination you can produce some very interesting and highly personal work with this simple technique.

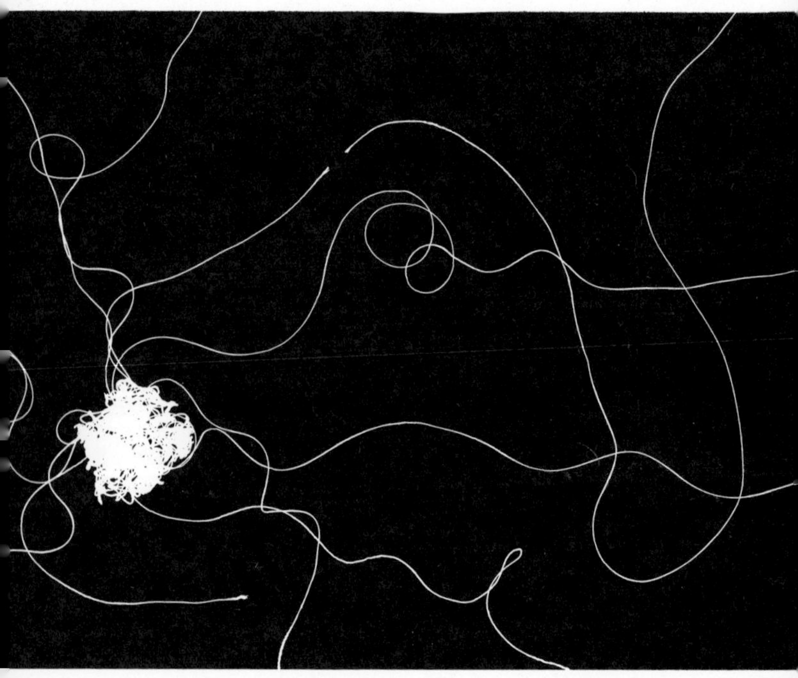

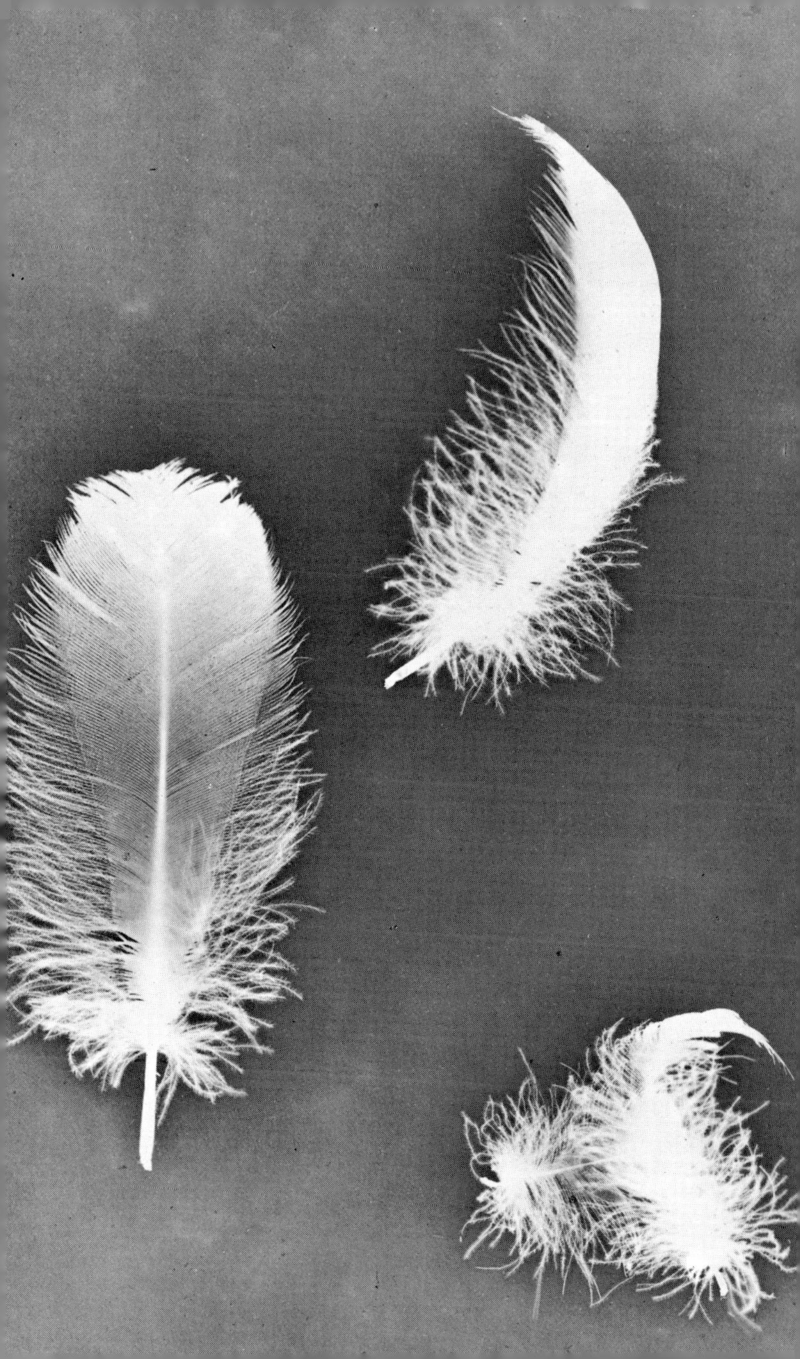

Rayograms
This technique was invented by the famous Bauhaus artist, Man Ray, which is the reason for its name.
It is a development of the foregoing method by which it is possible to obtain pictures of three-dimensional objects without a camera.
All you do is place transparent objects like glasses or plastic funnels, etc; on a piece of paper and expose in the same way as before. You can if you like take one of the objects away and then give the others a further exposure, so as to vary the grey tones. For this technique it is generally best to have the enlarger set up obliquely as shown in the illustration.

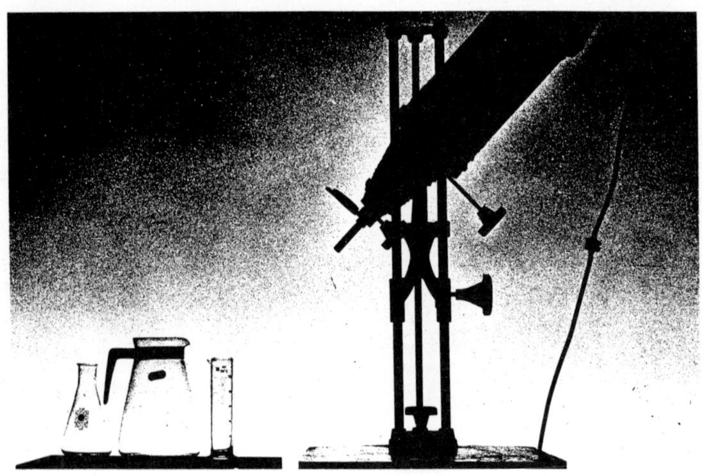

Cliché-verre
One of the best ways of obtaining the basic material for this very old photographic technique is to expose a piece of lith film to white light and then develop it right out to get a piece of dead black film.
You then take a good sharp needle (I always use a compass needle sharpened up on a whetstone) and scratch a picture or pattern into the black emulsion. You can sketch the outline first with a soft pencil without doing any damage. It helps if you can mount the film on a light-

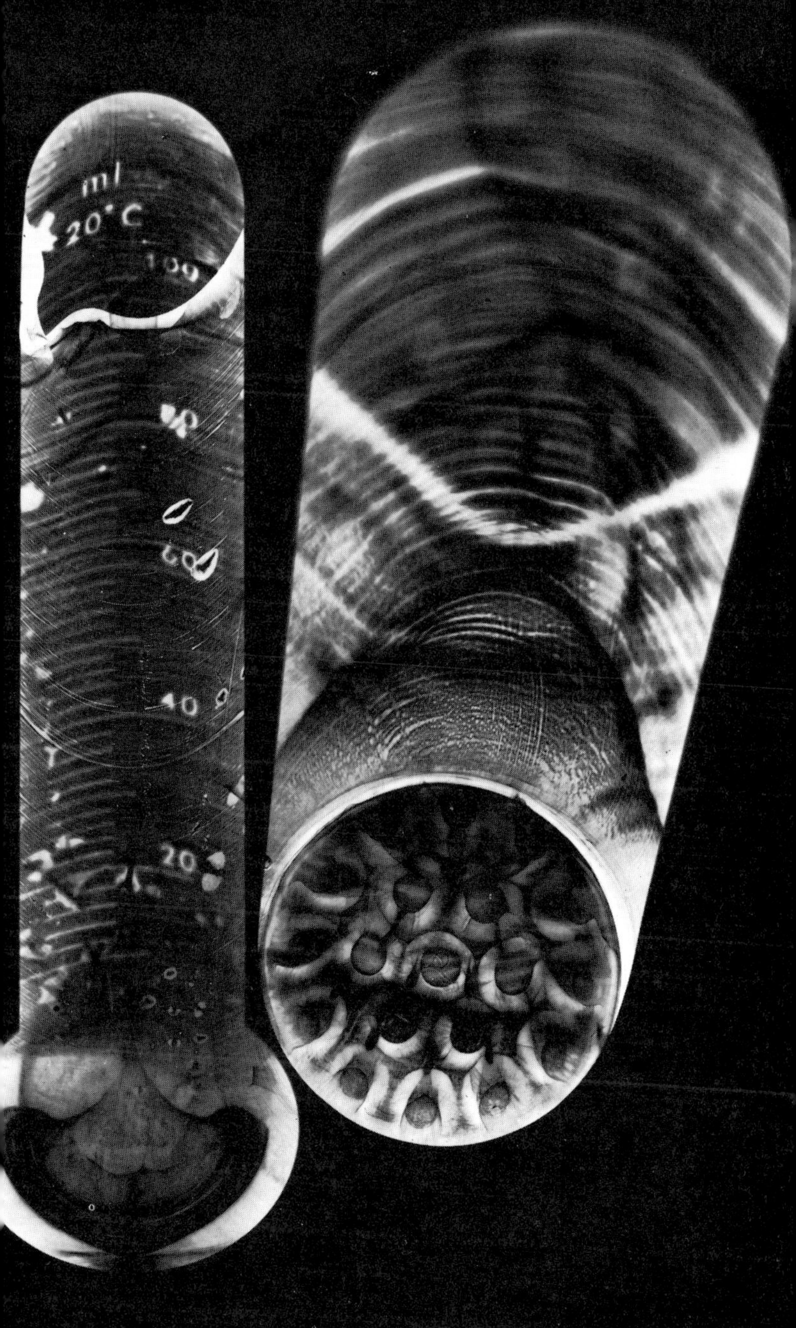
ml
20°C
100
40
20

box so that you can see what you are doing. If by any chance you make a mistake, you can always cover the area again with the retouching paint and then re-scratch when it dries.

When you are satisfied with your efforts you will have what is in effect a negative that you can go ahead and print in the normal way. Since it will be enlarged, probably about eight times, the scratched lines will have a particularly ragged look which is in fact typical of cliché-verre work and has an attraction of its own. In fact, the correct choice of magnification so that just the right amount of raggedness is obtained is vital to the success of this technique.

One further development is to use this technique on an existing negative to get a combined effect of tone and line.

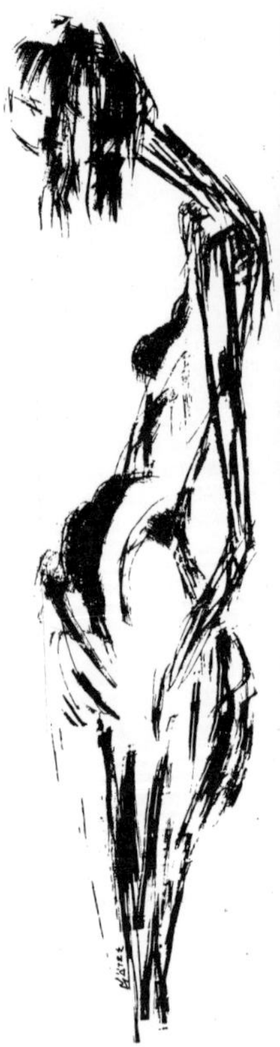

3. Lighting the subject

In general, photographic derivation is a branch of pictorial art used to produce in simple black and white a representation of a given image. This limitation has, if nothing else, the advantage that it makes it simple to divide the subject up into a series of lines and areas. We must therefore form a concept of essential contours, and the silhouette is a good example on which to work.

Outdoors: Choose a time of day when no direct sunlight is falling on the subject. If at all possible, choose a blue sky as a background and use a blue filter to make this background come out as dark as possible in the negative. Keep the exposure short, and print out on hard or extra-hard paper to emphasize the black-and-white contrast.

Indoors: Place a dark object in front of a light background or a light object in front of a dark background. In the former case, make sure the background is evenly lit but at the same time make sure that no light falls on the front of the subject. For light subjects, use diffused lighting coming from both sides so that one side of the subject will not come out darker than the other. Develop on the soft side but print out on hard or extra-hard paper as before.

Needless to say, any non-transparent object will come out looking black when photographed in this way.

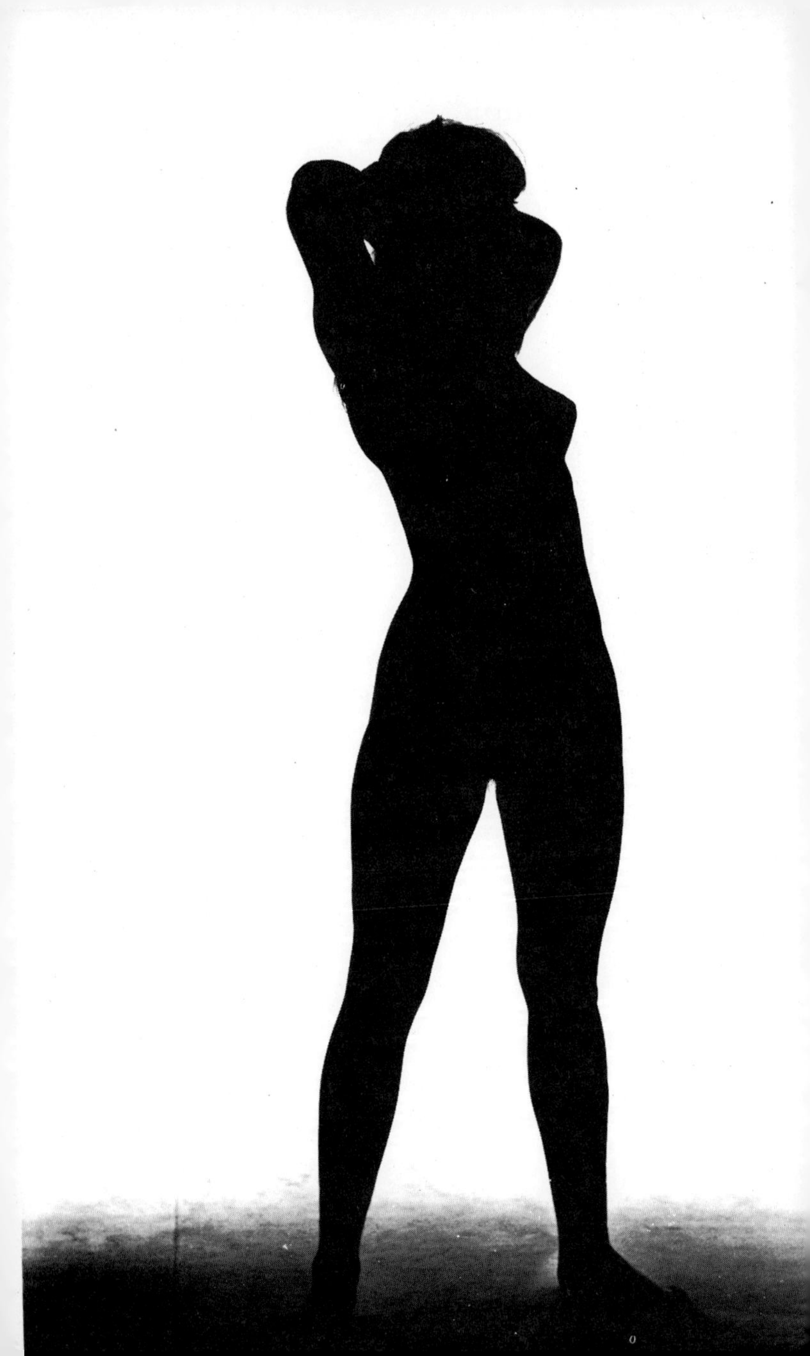

4. Preparing the subject

One thing I am always stressing is the importance of realizing that the success or otherwise of the final print begins at the very beginning – with the choice and treatment of subject. To put it another way, the first part of the graphic process lies in the preparation of the subject, so let us have a few words on that topic now.

One misunderstanding that I want to clear up first, however, is the idea that you need hard negatives to work from. Just the opposite, in fact. If you want to get rid of the intermediate tones it is best to start with a very soft negative.

The reason is quite clear if you think about it. The ultra-hard film that we use for this purpose has in fact a very small exposure latitude. In other words, when a certain exposure produces a deep black effect, another exposure which is only very slightly shorter will produce nothing at all. Now, if you use a hard negative to print from, it will already have quite wide separation of its tones and there will be appreciable differences between adjacent half-tones. This will mean that the detail in the shadows will be lost or, if the shadows are more than just black patches, the rest of the photograph will be hopelessly overexposed.

For the same reson you have to be careful with subject contrast, which is one aspect of subject preparation that I want to mention. Take, for instance, a standing figure lit from overhead with a single lamp. If this lamp is placed about 1 m above the model's head and the model is 1.7 m tall, then the feet will be getting only about half the light that the head is receiving. Put another way, it means that either the feet will be one stop underexposed or the head will be one stop overexposed.

With a normal half-tone film this difference is not especially important. You would expect it and therefore not notice it. But if the intermediate tones are removed, it means that either the model has no feet, because they are lost in a sea of ink, or she is completely without a head!

If you want to use the pseudo-solarization process or if you want to use Agfacontour film you will have to take special note of the shadow contours. It is these boundaries that form the solarization lines in the print.

Another process that has had a great deal of attention recently is the idea of equidensity, of which more later in Chapter 6. For the present, all I want to say is that this is one of the most interesting concepts in photographic derivation. Put very simply, they are lines of equal density rather like the lines of equal pressure (called isobars) that you see on the weather map. Therefore, if you remove the intermediate tones the boundaries between the areas that are left will in fact run

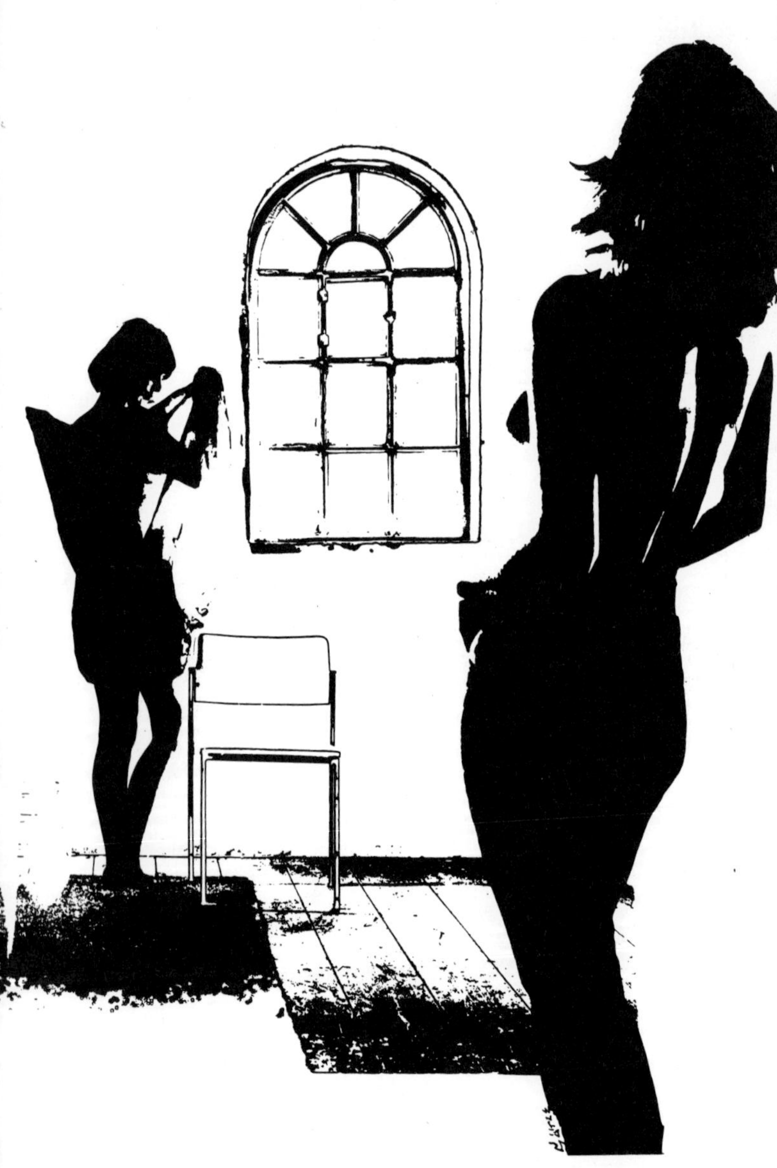

along these lines of equal density. The same applies with solarization or with the results produced by Agfacontour film.
This having been said, you will now realize that if the negative doesn't look the way you thought it would, it's no use blaming the material. What appears in the negative was there to be seen in the first place and how it gets there is a matter, not of luck, but of observation. Naturally, you must expect to make mistakes and to learn from them. You must observe closely the ways in which the negative deviates from your intentions and try to find out why. If you want it to come out black in the final print, that's the way it should come out.
Again, you can have problems when one part of the body is better lit than another. Eyebrows in a brightly-lit face will not come out as well as the veins in a hand that is lit only half as brightly. Of course this is a real problem if that is the only lighting available, or the only one that will produce the right amount of texture. Well, don't lose heart because there's always a way round these difficulties. For a start, as I have already remarked, the best negatives for derivatives work are soft; and you can employ some crafty fiddles during printing, of which more later (in Chapter 5, in fact).
Mind you, I have to say that in my opinion this is the inferior method. Not that I have anything against the use of darkroom techniques, but they can easily become substitutes for correct preparation which is the only right way of going about things – the better the initial negative, the better the final result.
What I aim for is a clear negative, developed to be a little on the soft side but sharply focused and with the minimum of grain clumping. Starting from something like this, there is virtually no limit to what you can achieve.
But what if you want a grainy effect? Well, in Chapter 5 there is a method given by which you can add grain to a photograph. There is another way and it involves making a perfect print from a perfect negative. You photograph this, using a very fast film and selecting a distance that will produce an image not more than about quarter of a 35 mm negative in area. Use a developer that brings out the grain – Rodinal will do the trick, as will Promicrol or Microphen – and then make an enlarged print. You will find that grain is a lot easier to add to a negative than it is to remove.

5. Removing half-tones

Strangely enough, one of the main features of photography can also be one of its disadvantages. This is the amount of detail that is normally incorporated into a photograph.
It can therefore be useful to remove some of this detail and it is one of the functions of derivation processes to do this. One way of removing detail from a photograph is to get rid of the half-tones so as to produce an effect rather reminiscent of a pen-and-ink drawing, a composition of lines and surfaces.

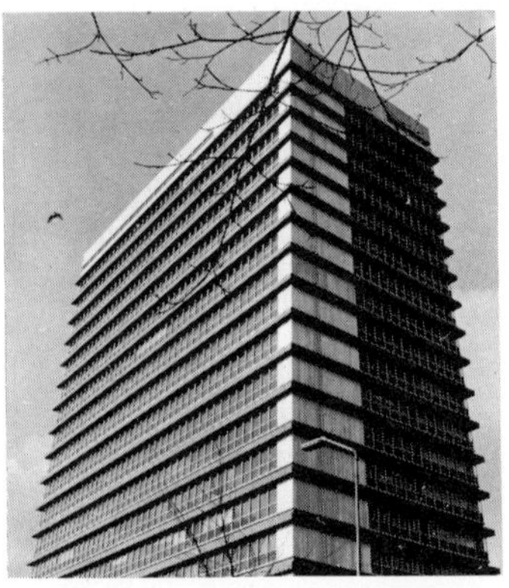

First stage

Method
Stage One: Print the initial negative on to an ultra-hard film such as Kodalith.
Stage Two: Copy the diapositive you obtain in this way on to another piece of the same material to produce a negative.
Stage Three: Copy it again to produce yet another positive, now virtually without half-tones.
Stage Four: One further copying will produce a negative completely free of half-tones from which the final print can be made.
As the illustration shows, the final print has all the characteristics of a line drawing.

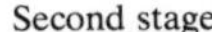

Second stage

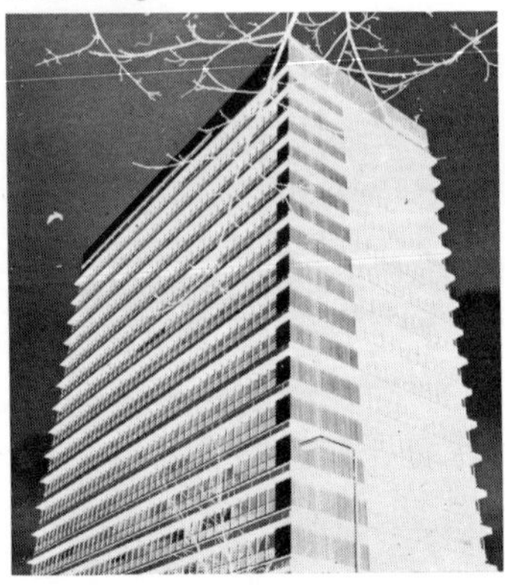

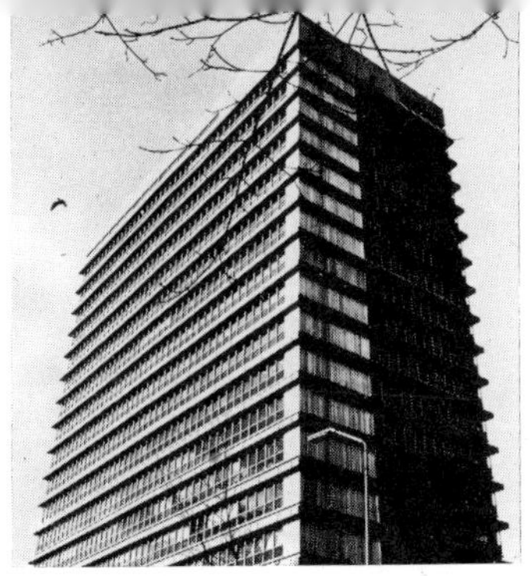

Third stage

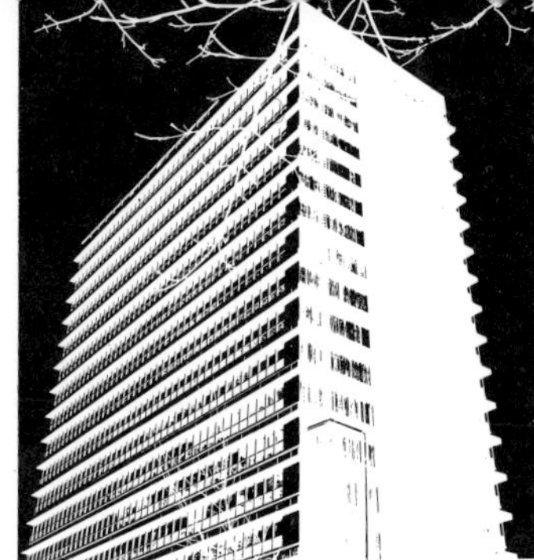

Fourth stage

Final result

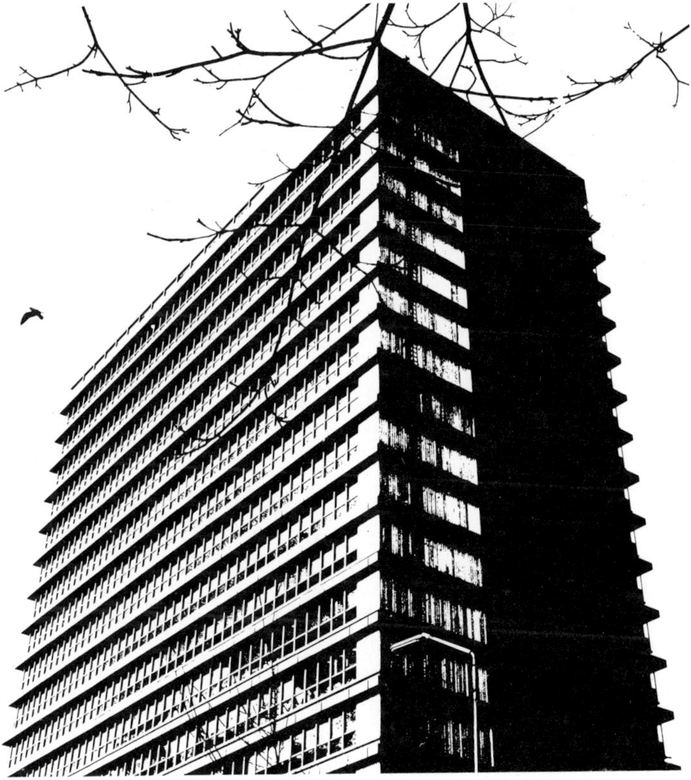

Applying grain.
Sometimes you don't want the background to be completely blank. In such cases, you can give a hint of a half-tone by putting in some grain.
Stage One: Make a diapositive on to hard film material. During this exposure a sheet of course ground glass is placed in close contact with the diapositive. The grade of coarseness of the glass is something you will have to work out by experiment.
Stage Two: Copy this positive on to another piece of hard film to make a negative.
Stage Two: Copy again to get another diapositive. By this time the background grain should be fading somewhat.
Stage Four: Same as the third stage with the grain etched out from parts of the face and background.

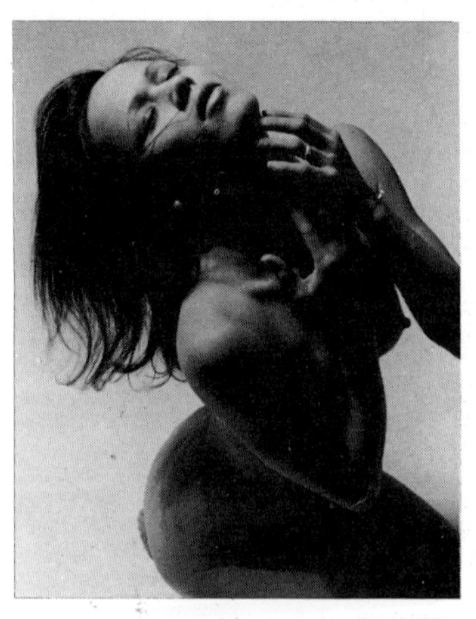

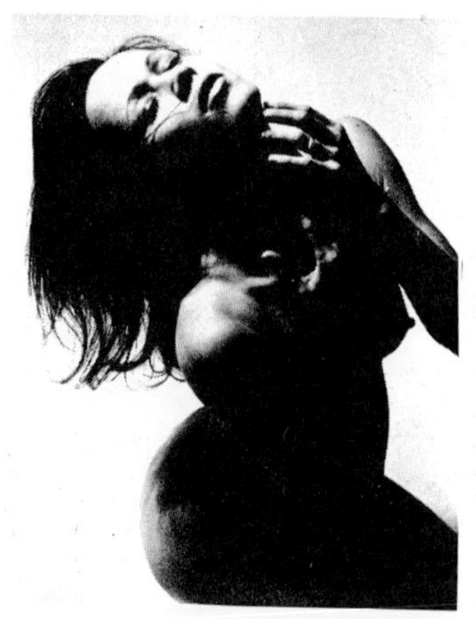

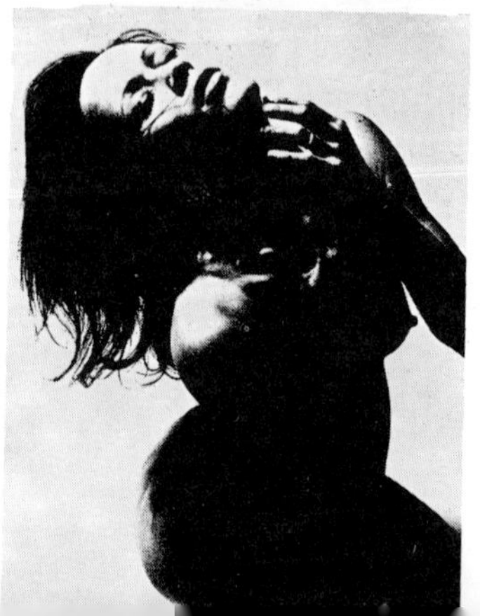

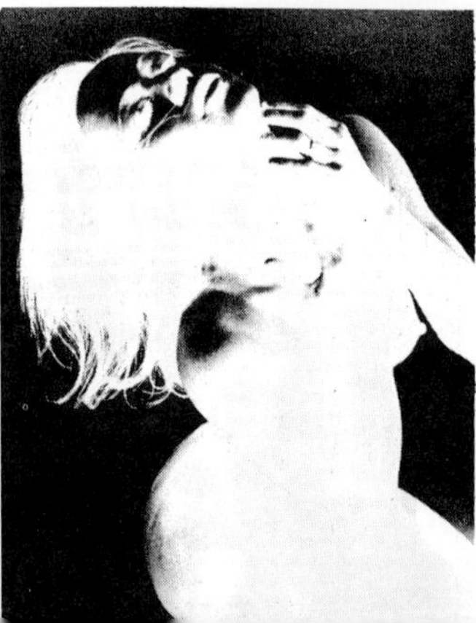

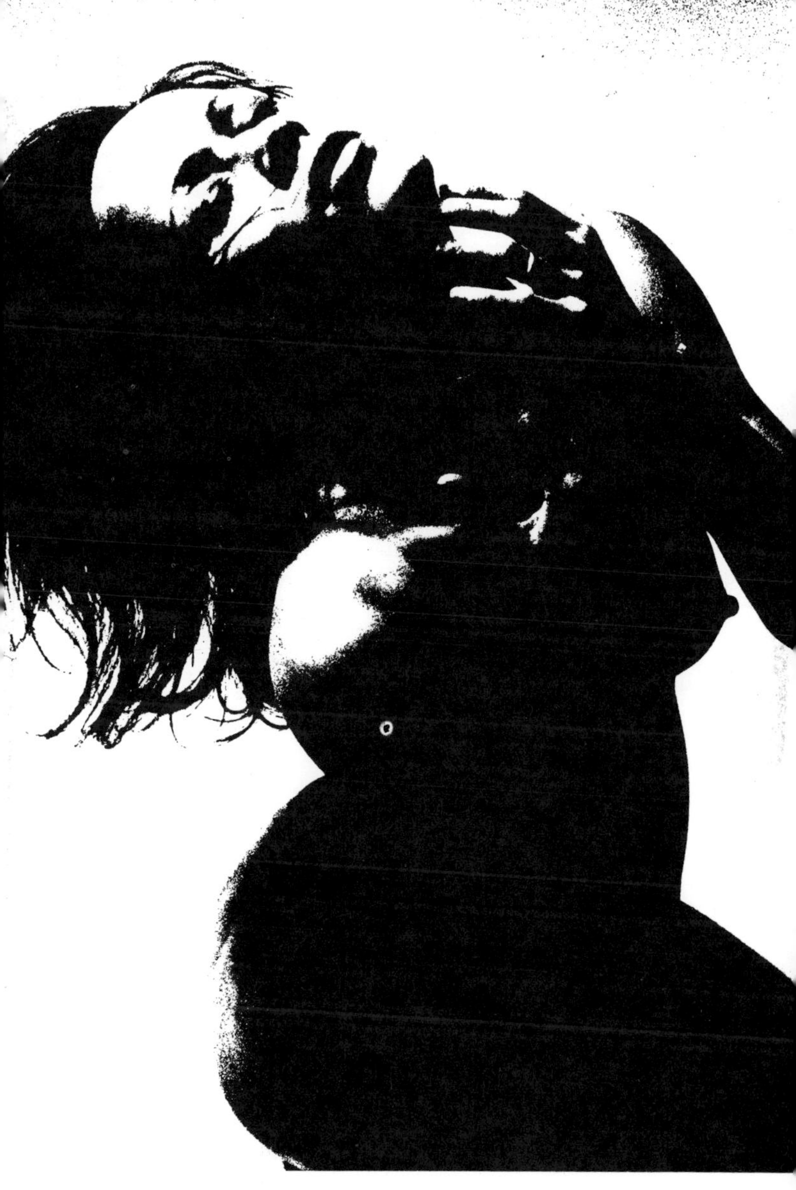

6. Equidensities

As the name implies, equidensities are points or areas in a negative at which the density is the same. These points can be joined up to form lines of equal density which are rather like the lines of equal pressure (called isobars) that you see on a weather map, or the lines of equal height (normally referred to as contours) on a map of hilly ground.
In the examples given in Chapter 5, the boundaries between black and white areas follow equidensity lines precisely. Now, if such a line surrounds an area of a given density, then an increase in exposure will make the area larger and hence will move the position of the line. In the same way, a shorter exposure will reduce the area, so moving the line the other way.
Referring back, you will recall that in Chapter 4 I had a few words to say on the subject of getting the right lighting to ensure that the contrast over the extent of the model was as constant as possible. Those parts of your subject that you wish to reproduce as white must all receive the same amount of light. Similarly the parts you want to come out black should have at least one light value (a stop or whatever other unit you are using) less illumination.
In the illustration you will see that areas are divided by a white line or band. This line follows the contour which divides areas of one density from those of another. You will realize that different negatives can have this line in different places and you can see the results of superimposing several of these negatives on p 38.

Pseudo-solarization; the Sabattier effect

Pseudo-solarization is an effect that occurs when a partly-developed film is exposed to white light. The result is part negative and part positive. In particular, the dark areas are surrounded by a white band which has a characteristically ragged look.
This effect is by no means as chancy as many people think. If you work out an exact method and follow it to the letter, the results are quite repeatable. One factor often ignored is the temperature of the developer – constant temperature is critical to the success of this method. Another factor which must be carefully controlled is the distance between the white light source and the surface of the negative.

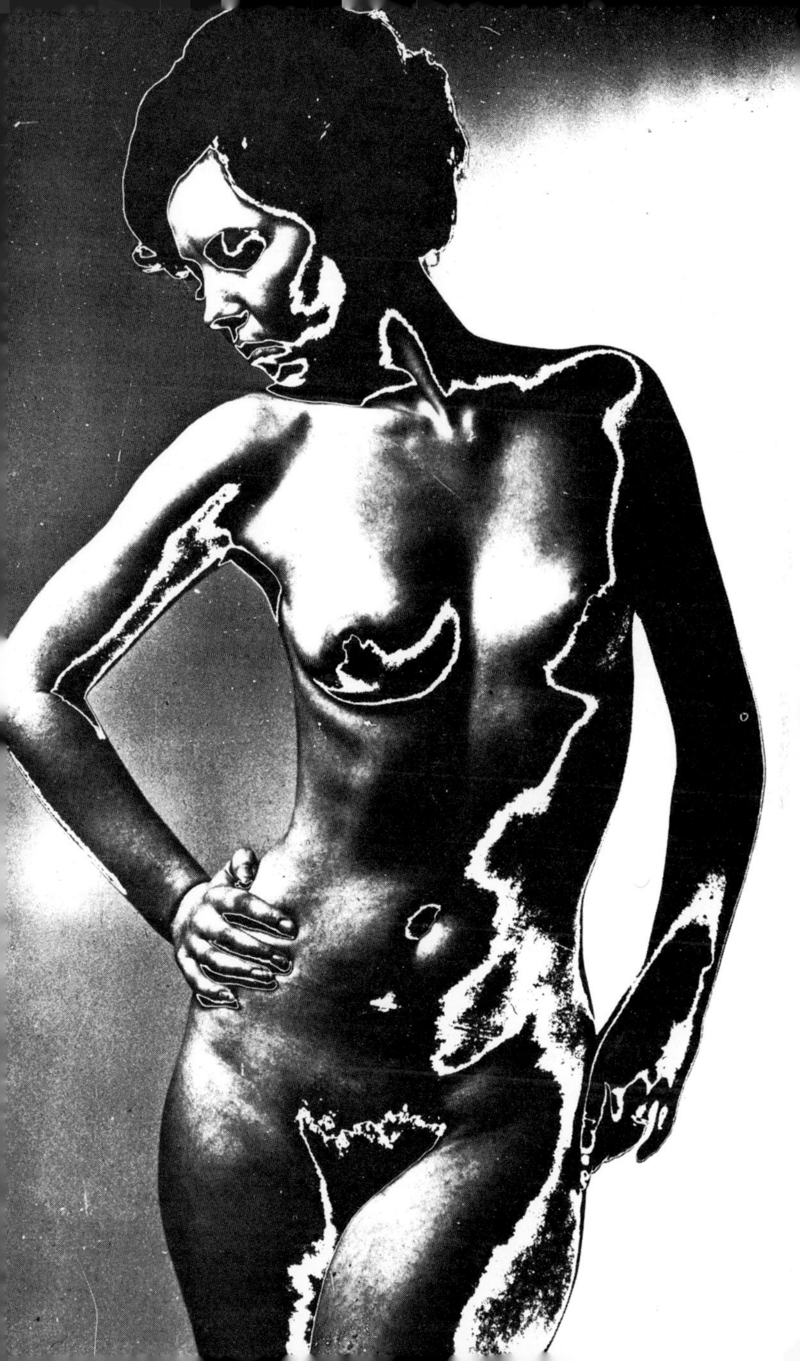

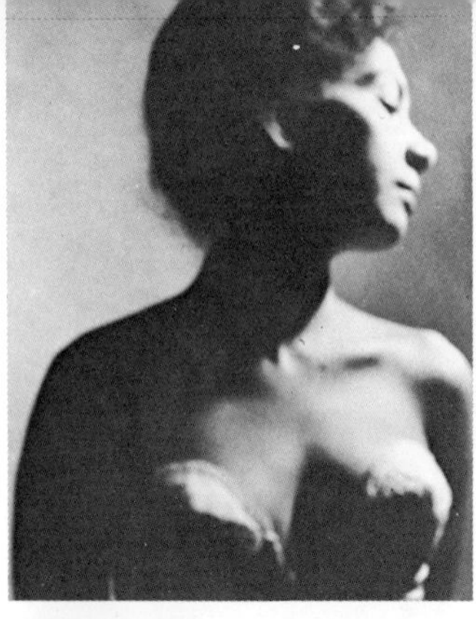

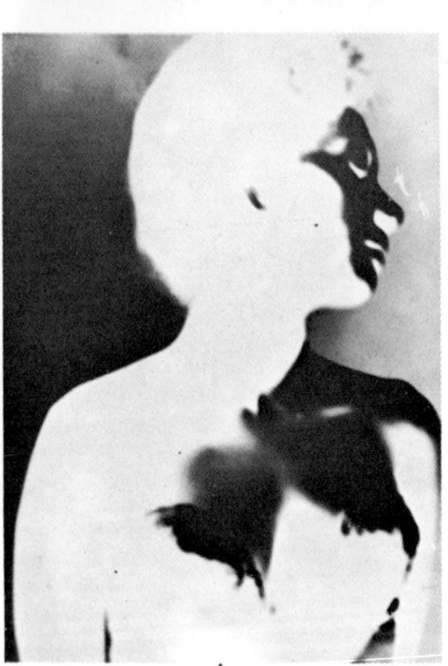

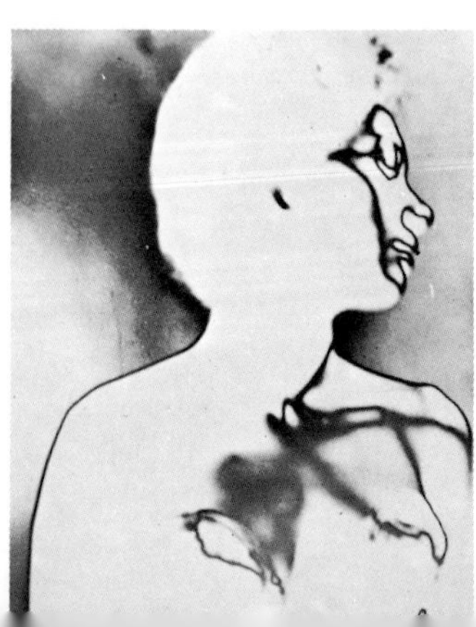

Method
The photograph used in these examples was deliberately taken out of focus. The subject distance was 1.5m, but the camera was focused at infinity. The lighting was deliberately harsh because this gives the best effect with solarization.

Stage One. The negative is copied on to extra-hard film.

Stage Two. Another copy is made on to extra-hard film by contact. A long exposure is given and the exposure to white light is provided by a 15-watt bulb set 60 cm from the surface of the film and switched on for between one and four seconds. The exact moment for this white-light exposure has been reached when the rear face of the film has attained a medium grey tone, which will normally be between 30 and 45 seconds from the start of development. The film is then developed for a further 30 sec. The illustration shown here is a print taken from this piece of film.

Stage Three. The whole process is then repeated. The second stage is again printed on to extra-hard film and treated as above. The print taken from this film shows a double line.

The process can be repeated yet again if desired.

For more information about pseudo-solarization see page 91.

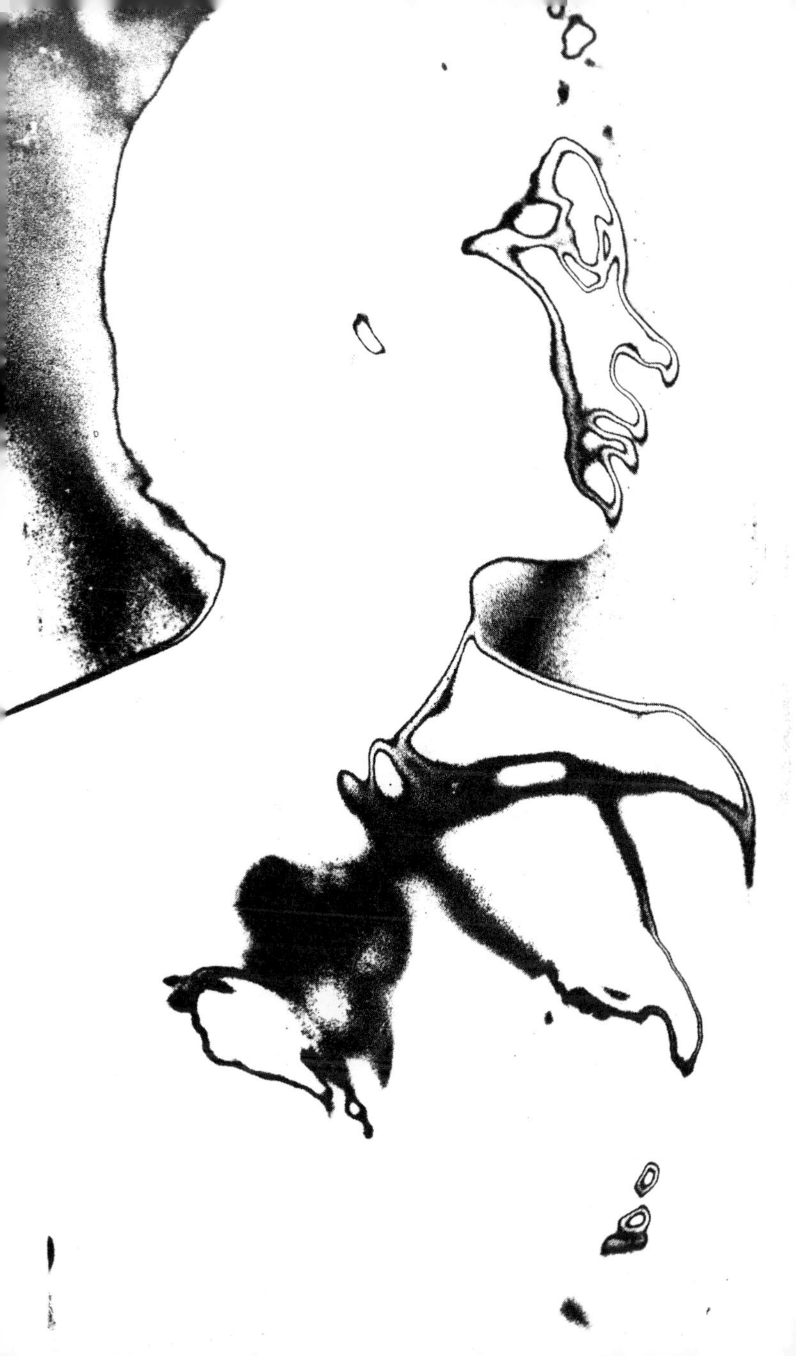

Superimposition

You can if you wish vary the density in a negative to obtain different patterns of equidensity lines. These lines may then be superimposed in a single print to give a more complex pattern.

Method using pseudo-solarization

Stage One: from a soft and clear diapositive, make four negatives using different exposures. In general, doubling the exposure time in each case will produce the necessary degree of difference between them. The aim should be to have shadow details in the print from the longest exposure that are not visible in the shortest one.

Stage Two: Make pseudo-solarizations from these negatives.

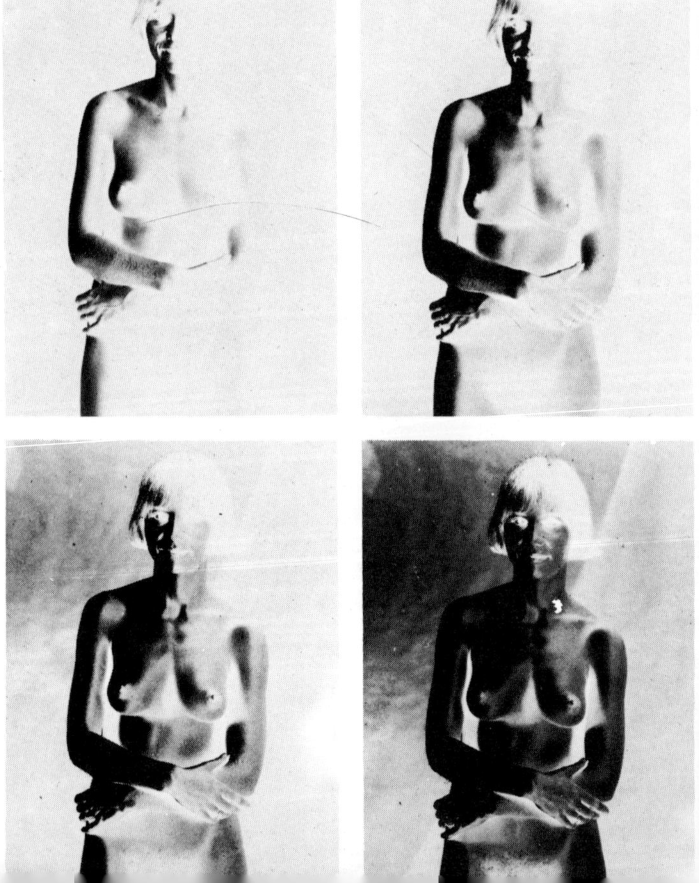

Registering prints

Soak a piece of bromide paper in developer for about a minute, then lay it on a sheet of glass and wipe the excess moisture off it.

Take the first of the solarized negatives from the second stage, put it in the enlarger and expose it on to the wet paper. Watch for the appearance of the image caused by the developer which remains in the paper emulsion, and then replace the first negative with the second. Using the red filter on the enlarger, you can line up the contours of the second negative with those of the developing latent image from the first negative and then continue the exposure. The same is done for the other two solarized negatives, and the paper is then further developed until a result similar to that shown on p 32 is obtained.

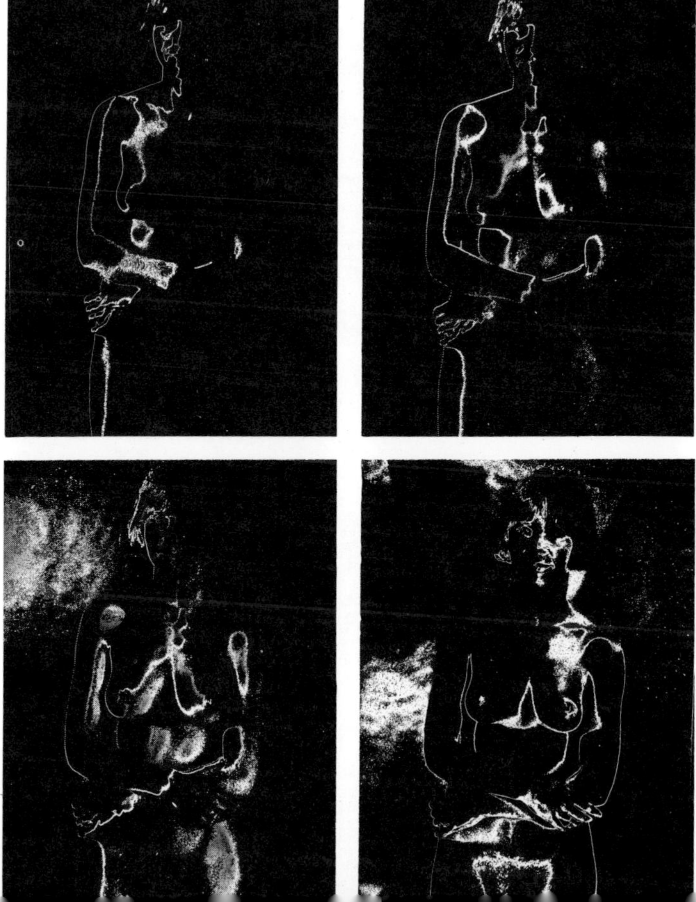

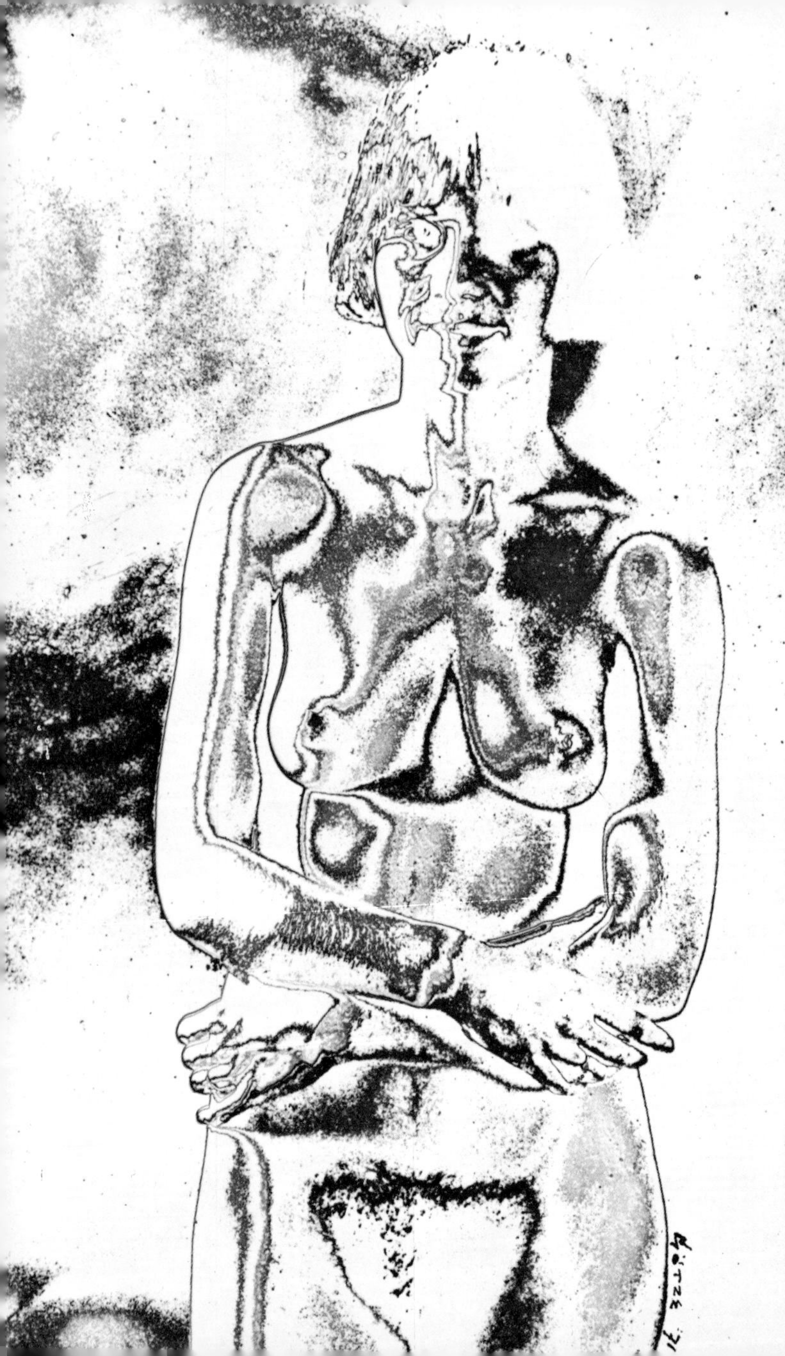

It is not necessary to get the negatives precisely in register and you need not use all four negatives. Sometimes it is better to use only two of them, thereby producing a less complicated and therefore somewhat more restful result. The illustration shows this effect and the print overleaf illustrates the effect of using only one negative and deliberately moving it during exposure.

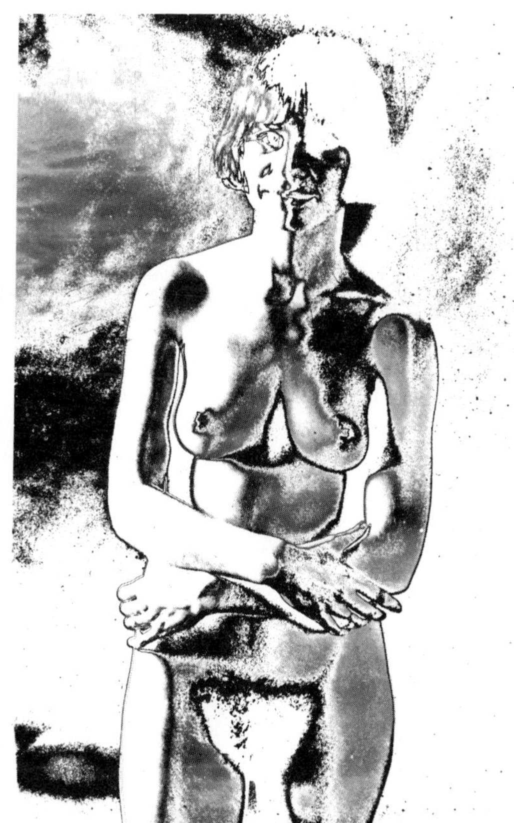

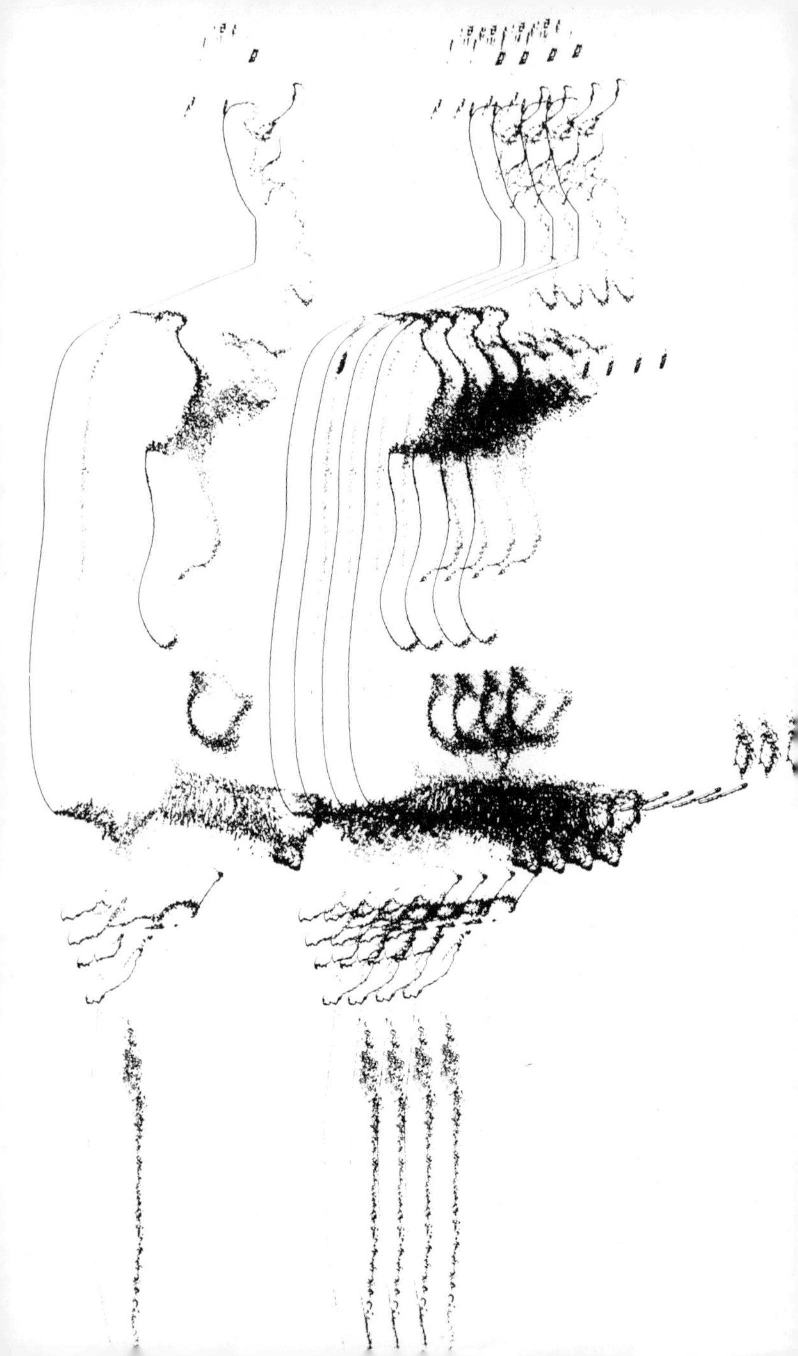

Agfacontour professional film

This is where you forget everything you ever learned about photography!

Agfacontour professional film breaks all the rules. This film goes black if you give it a short exposure in the developer and also goes black if you give it a long exposure. With a medium exposure you get a pretty weak diapositive, whereas with a shorter exposure you get a negative. As if that were not enough, with a slightly longer than average exposure you get a good diapositive and with a yet longer exposure again you get negative and positive combined on the same film!

All the effects described in this book can be attained by using Agfacontour which has some advantages and some disadvantages. One problem is that with such an unusual emulsion, you need a pretty unusual developer. However, let's take a practical example and see how it works.

Method

Stage One: Make a hard line-negative on Agfacontour. Use a 50:-:- yellow filter to control the line width. This will produce an equidensity of the first order.

Stage Two: If this is then printed on N81p, a reversed image is formed. By using longer or shorter exposures the line width can be varied, even though there is only one type of line in the first-stage film.

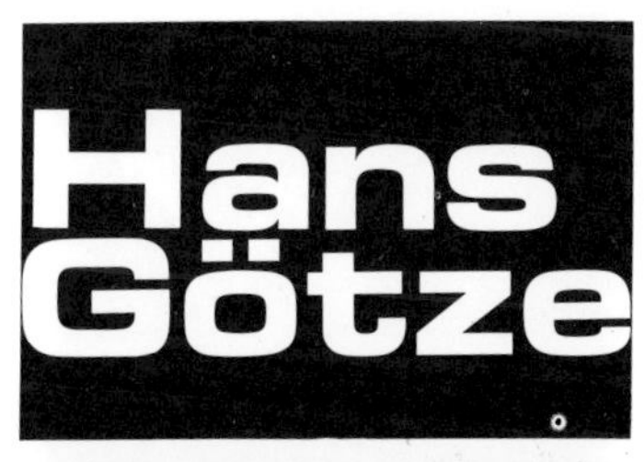

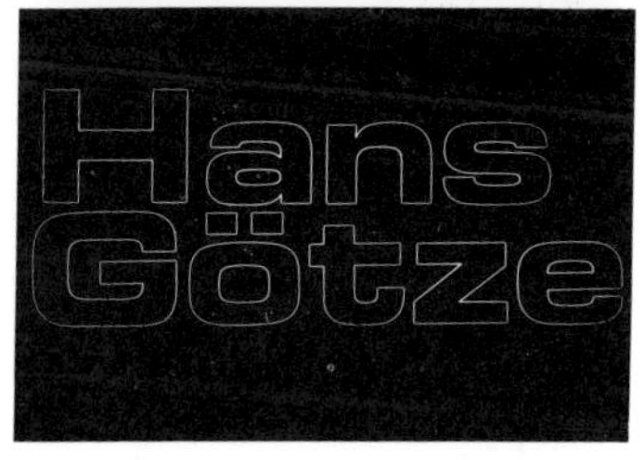

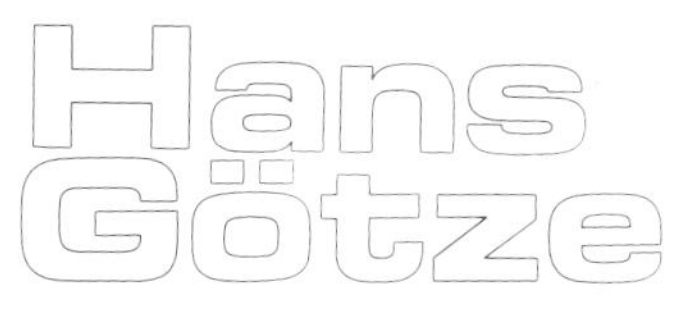

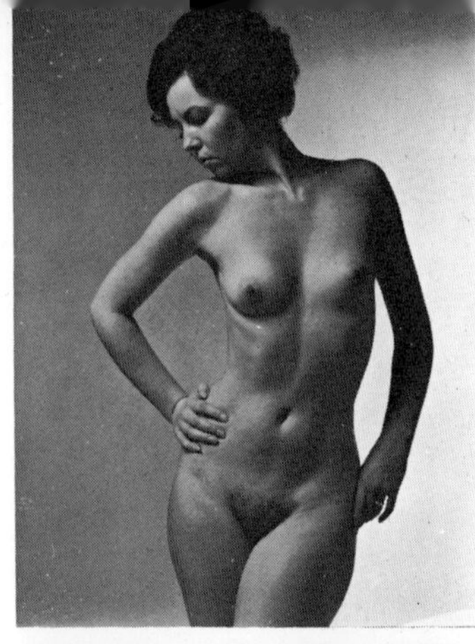

1

Method with contour film
Stage One: Make a good diapositive to start off with.

Stage Two: Make four negatives from this at different exposures.

Stage Three: Make contact prints from these negatives on contour film. The advantage of doing this rather than using solarization is that the line width can be closely controlled. In the cases illustrated,

2

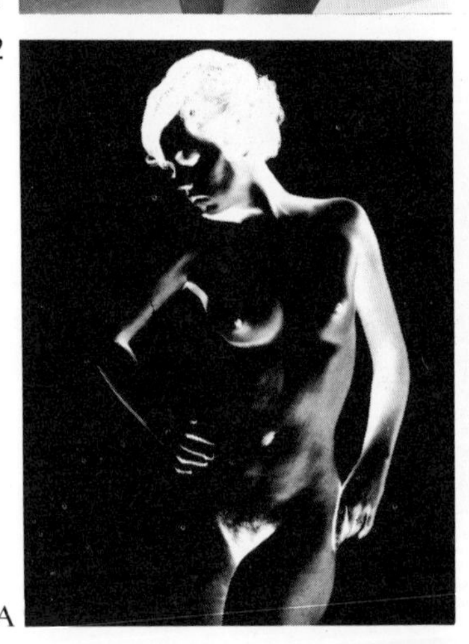

A

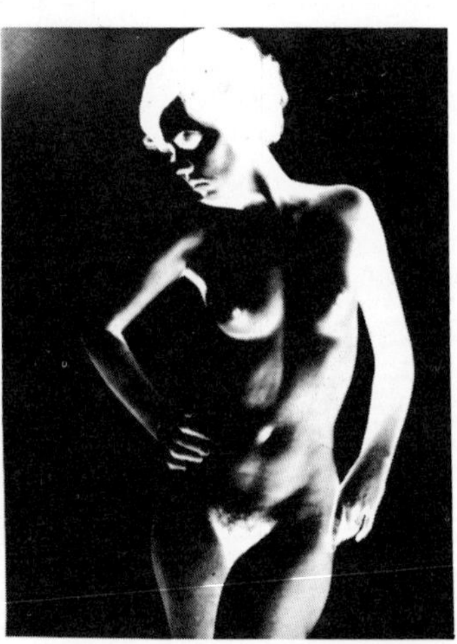

B

C

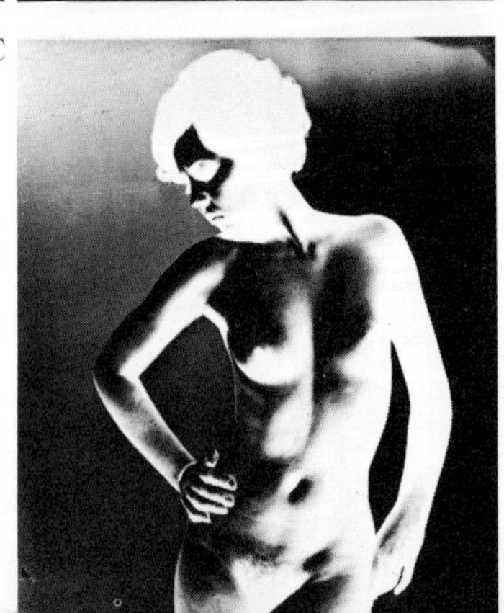

D

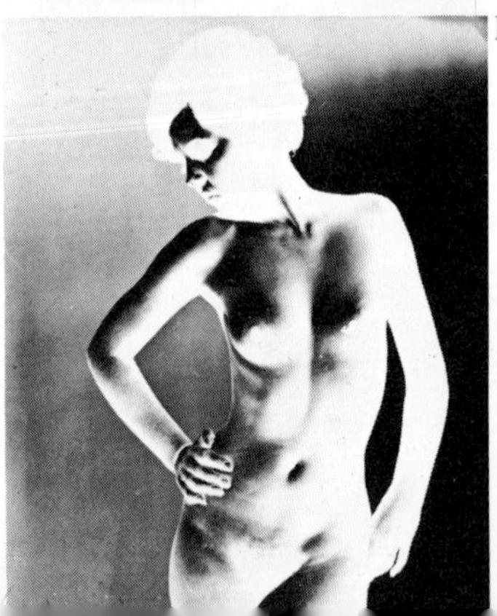

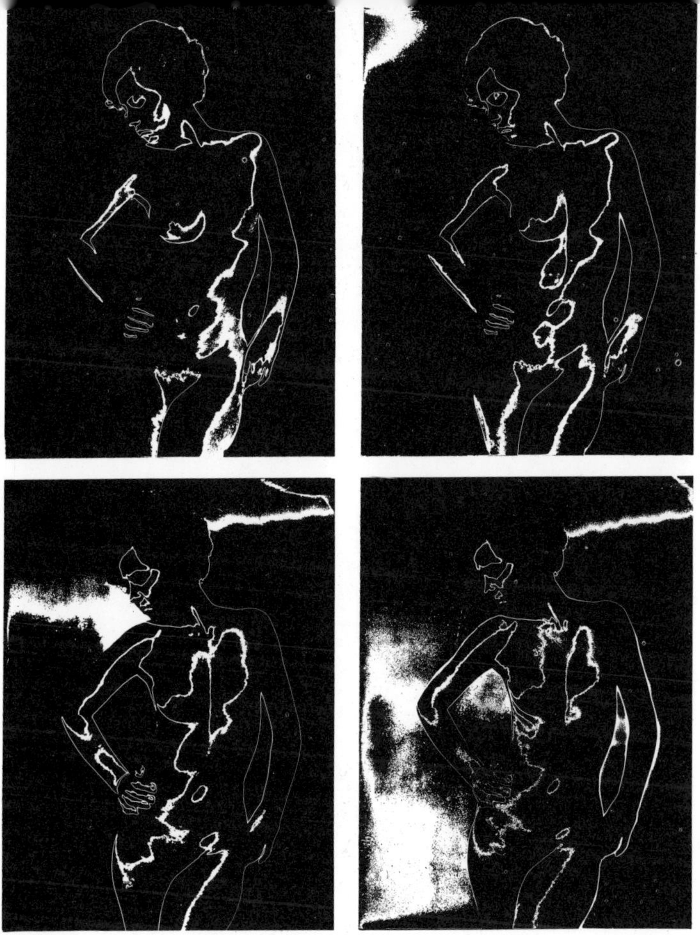

A

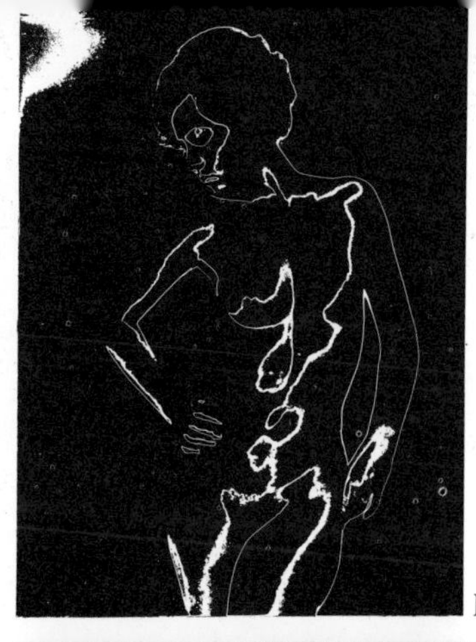

B

C

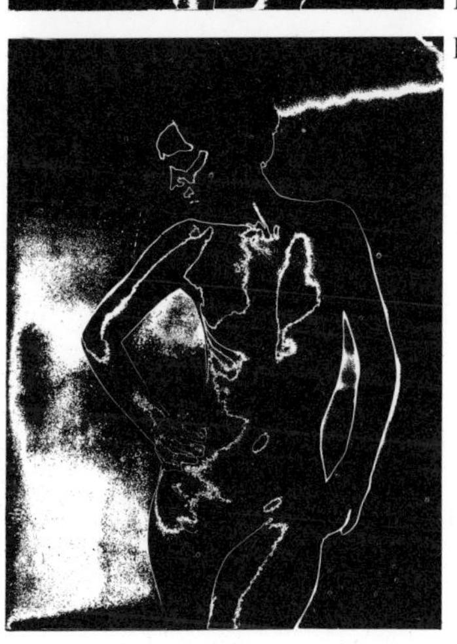

D

3

4

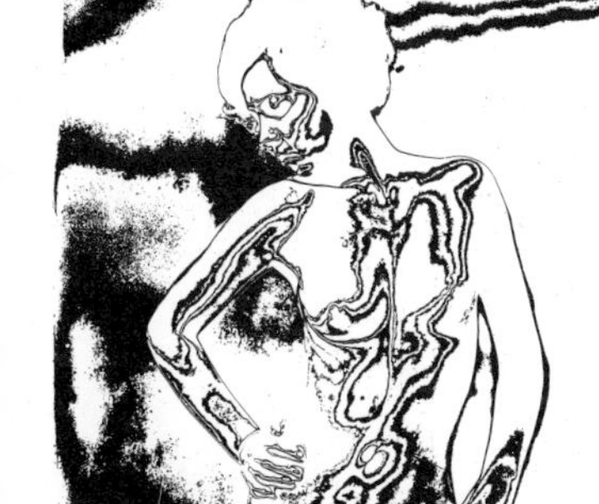

yellow filters of the following values were used:
A: 50:-:- ; B: 100:-:- ; C: 150:-:- ; D: 190:-:- . All prints at all stages should be perforated so that they can be accurately aligned for superimposition later.

Stage Four: Superimpose third stage negatives and print on to N8lp. The results of this are shown overleaf.

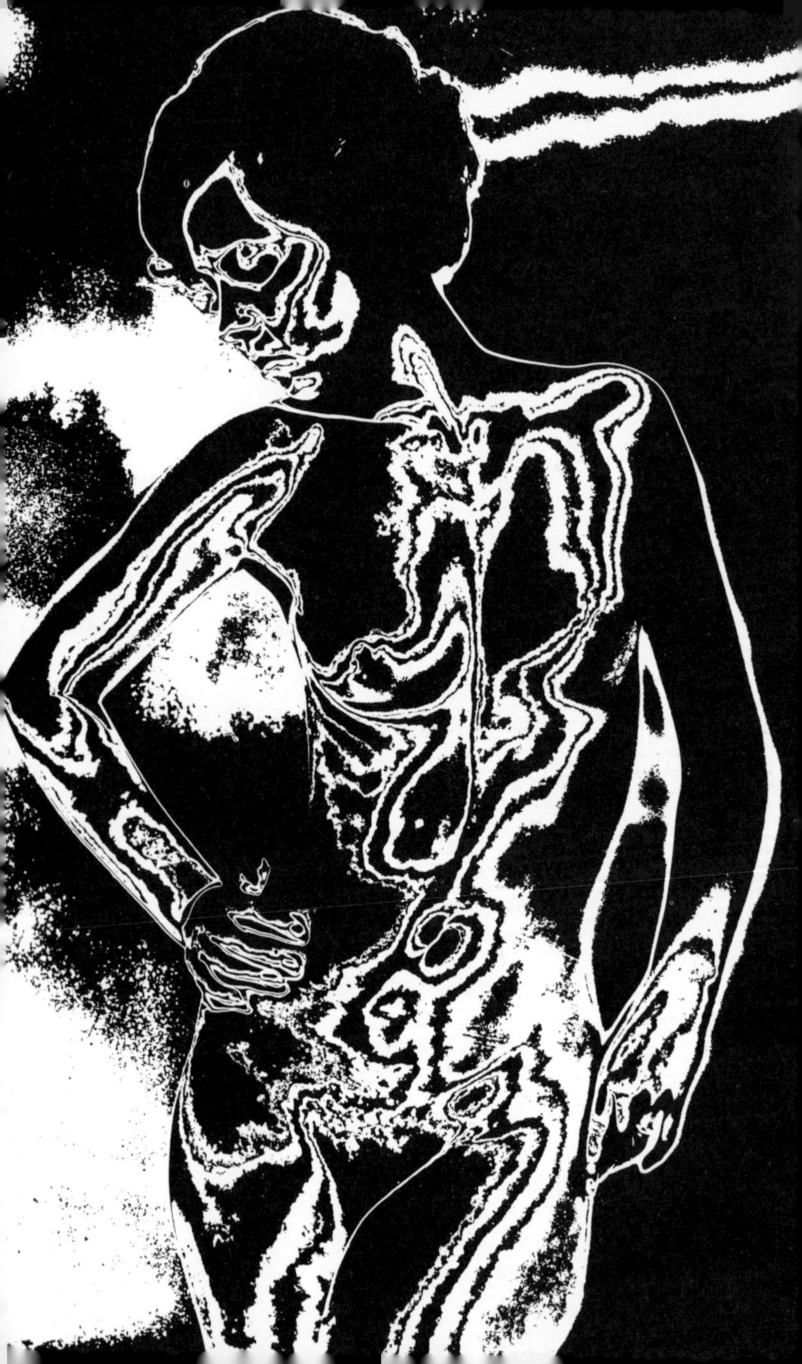

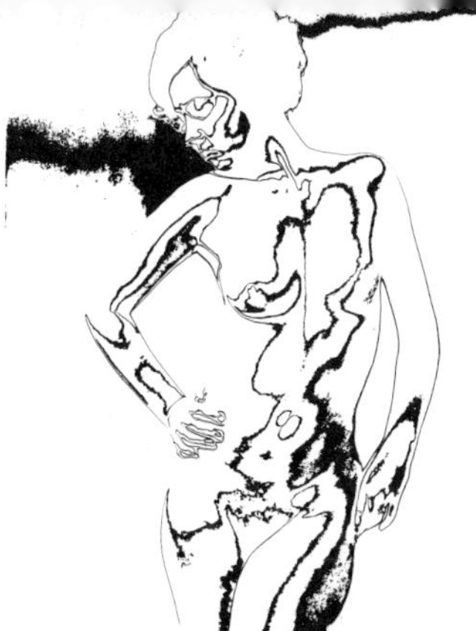

For further information about the finishing of Agfa contour film see page 92 onwards.

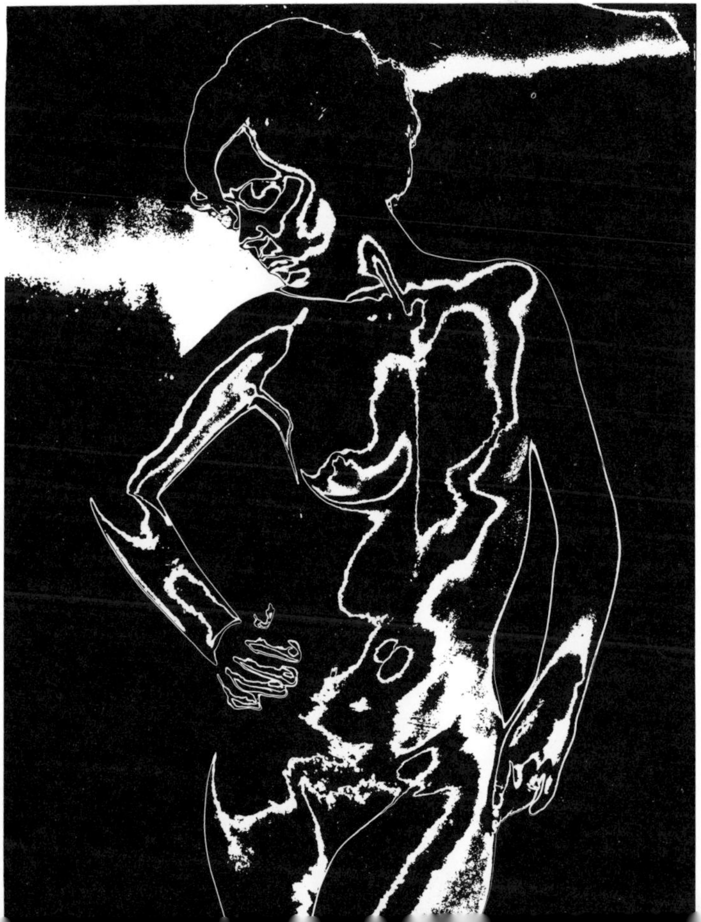

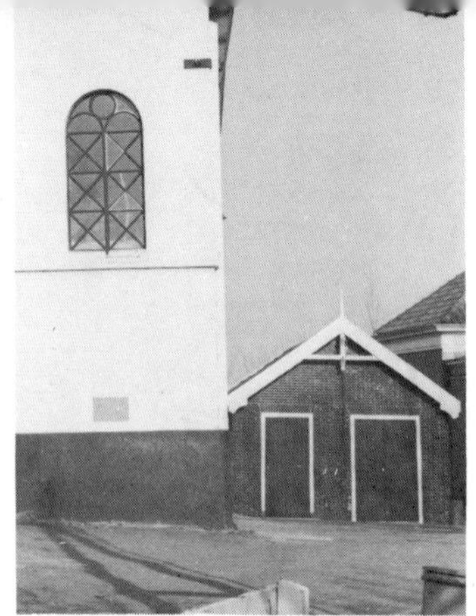

1

Combinations

Method

Stage One: Make a diapositive on N33p, perforated.

Stage Two: Make prints on contour film using varying exposures and a 50:-:- filter.

2

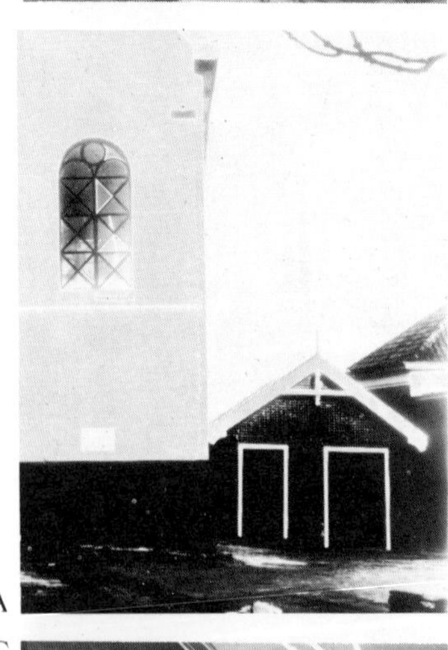

A

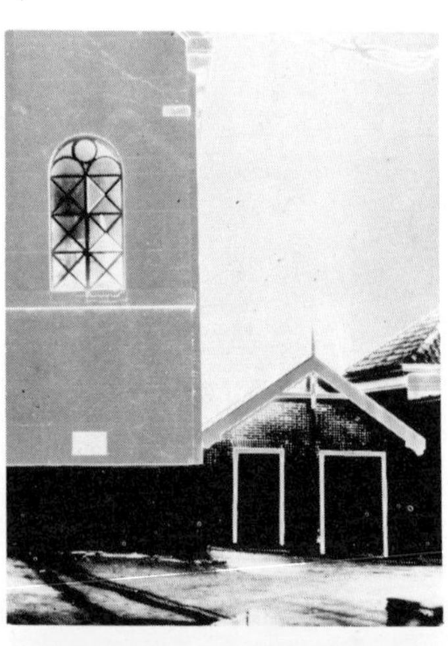

B

C

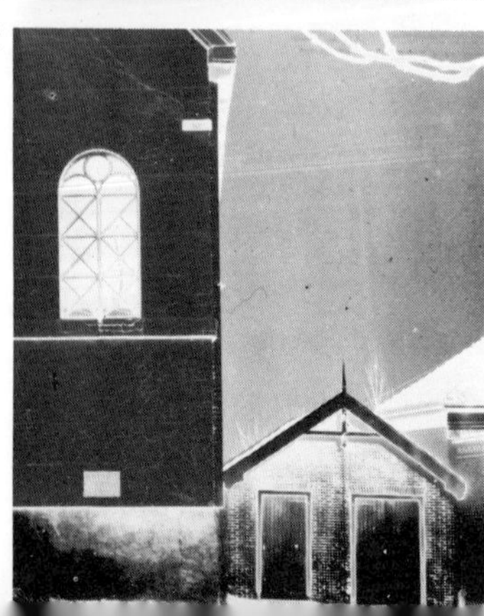

D

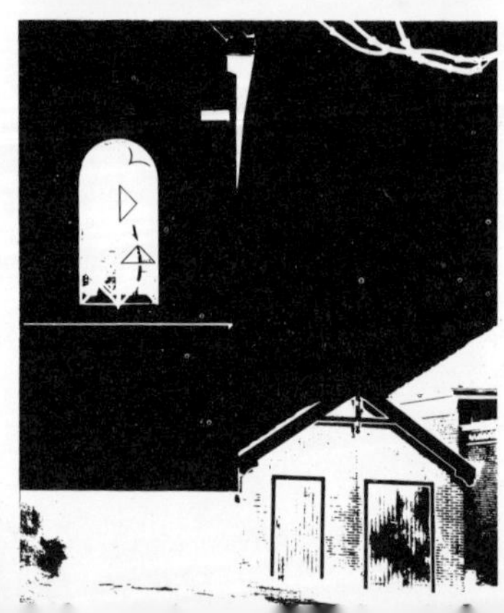

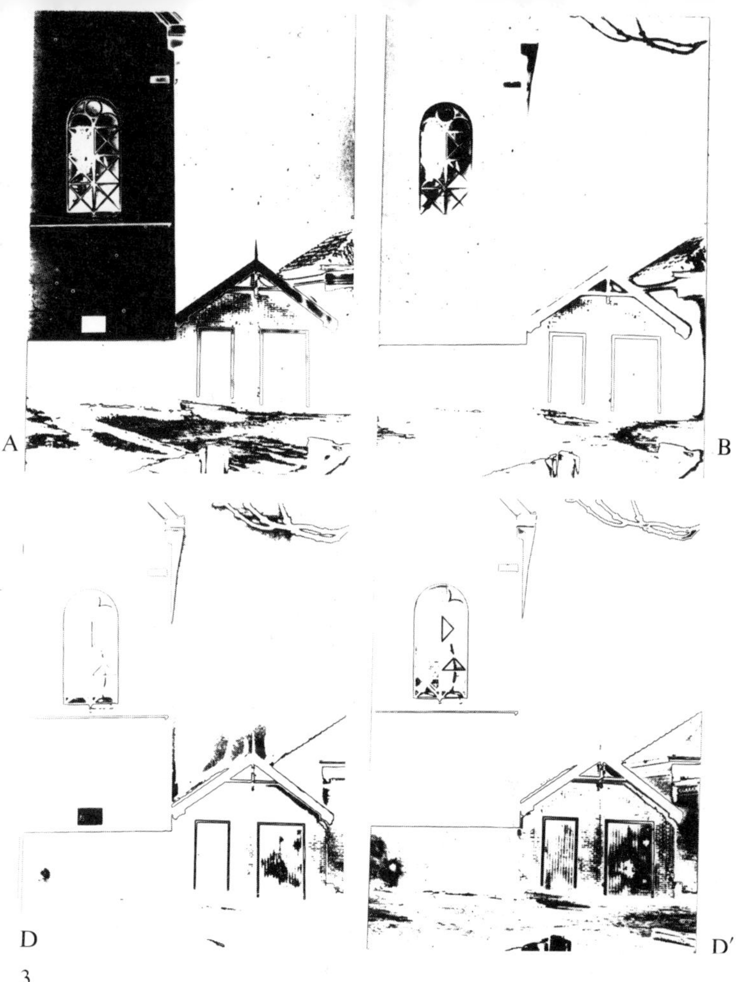

Stage Three: Copy A, B and D on to contour film. Example C in this case adds nothing to the process and can therefore be discarded. On the other hand, D can be printed at two different exposures, D and D^1, with good effect.

Reproduced are unretouched prints from these negatives. The next step is to take out the details which would overlap or which contribute nothing to the final result; use red retouching paint for this. You must develop an eye for detail because this step is vital.

Stage Four: Superimpose and print the four negatives on to the same piece of film. Examples 1, 2 and 3 are prints made to check the effect of retouching (see dotted lines). The final version is shown in 4, and the full size print of this is given on p 43.

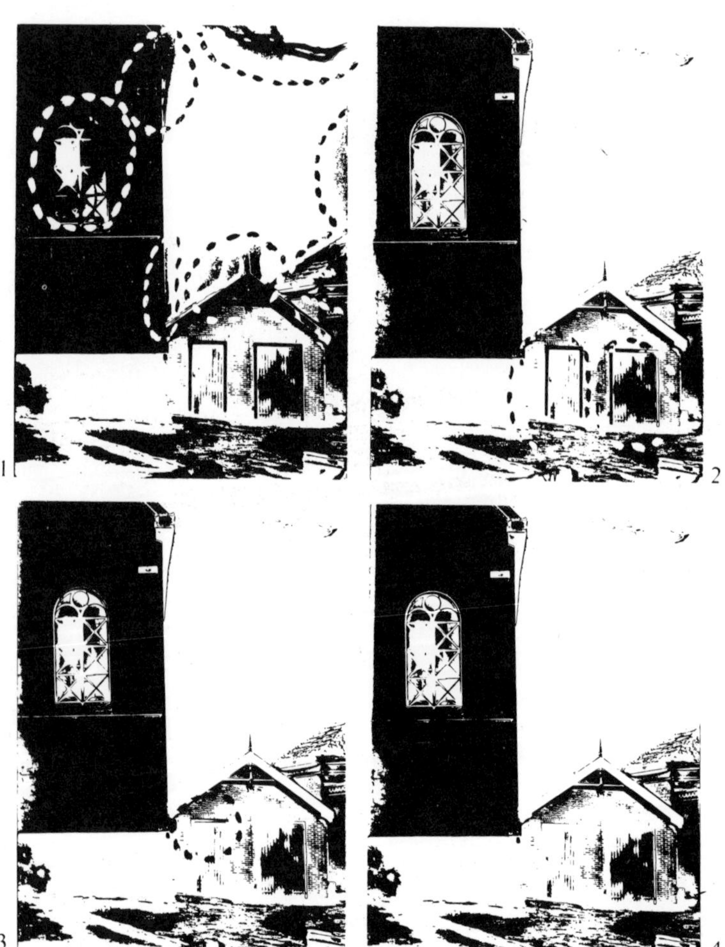

7. Line derivations

The main disadvantages of both pseudo-solarization and contour film are that they both tend to lose a lot of detail, and also that they are difficult to control so that results tend to be unpredictable. Also, the particular effect created by these processes, while impressive enough at times, is certainly not suitable for every subject.

Finally, and perhaps most important of all, it can be that the negative you want to use is not one that is suitable for the application of these techniques. For these reasons and in these cases, the auto-line or tone-line procedure of Kodak can be very useful in derivation work.

Method

Stage One: Starting with a normal negative, make a positive on film and make sure that it is not too small.

Stage Two: Make a contact print from this on to the same type of film and try to make sure that the contrast and density are as near to the positive as possible. The material used in the example shown was O8lp.

Stage Three: Place the positive and negative prints made in the previous two stages back-to-back, so as to make a sandwich. There are further notes on this process in the Appendix.

It is worth noting at this point that if you look at this sandwich directly you will only see a black piece of film because one print is (or should be) the exact opposite of the other. However, if you look at it a little to one side you will see that the separation caused by the thickness of the film is enough to make a white line visible around the edges of the various areas of density in the photograph. The further apart the two prints are set, the wider this line will look. It is this effect that we are going to exploit in the remaining stages of this process.

Stage Four: Place the sandwich in contact with another piece of film (O8l was used in our examples), and put the whole thing on some surface that can be rotated. A gramophone turntable is ideal but you can in fact make any old platter rotate around one point and it will do the job. The main object is to get light around all the edges of the dense areas.

You can use your enlarger as a light source but it has to be set at an angle of 45° so that the light falls obliquely on the sandwich of films on the turntable. If the enlarger cannot be set at this angle, use a spotlight. You should give a good long exposure while at the same time rotating the turntable so that light is received by the subject all round. When you develop the print made in this way you will get dark lines on a light background and, of course, a print made directly from that will have white lines against a dark ground, so you will need to go through this

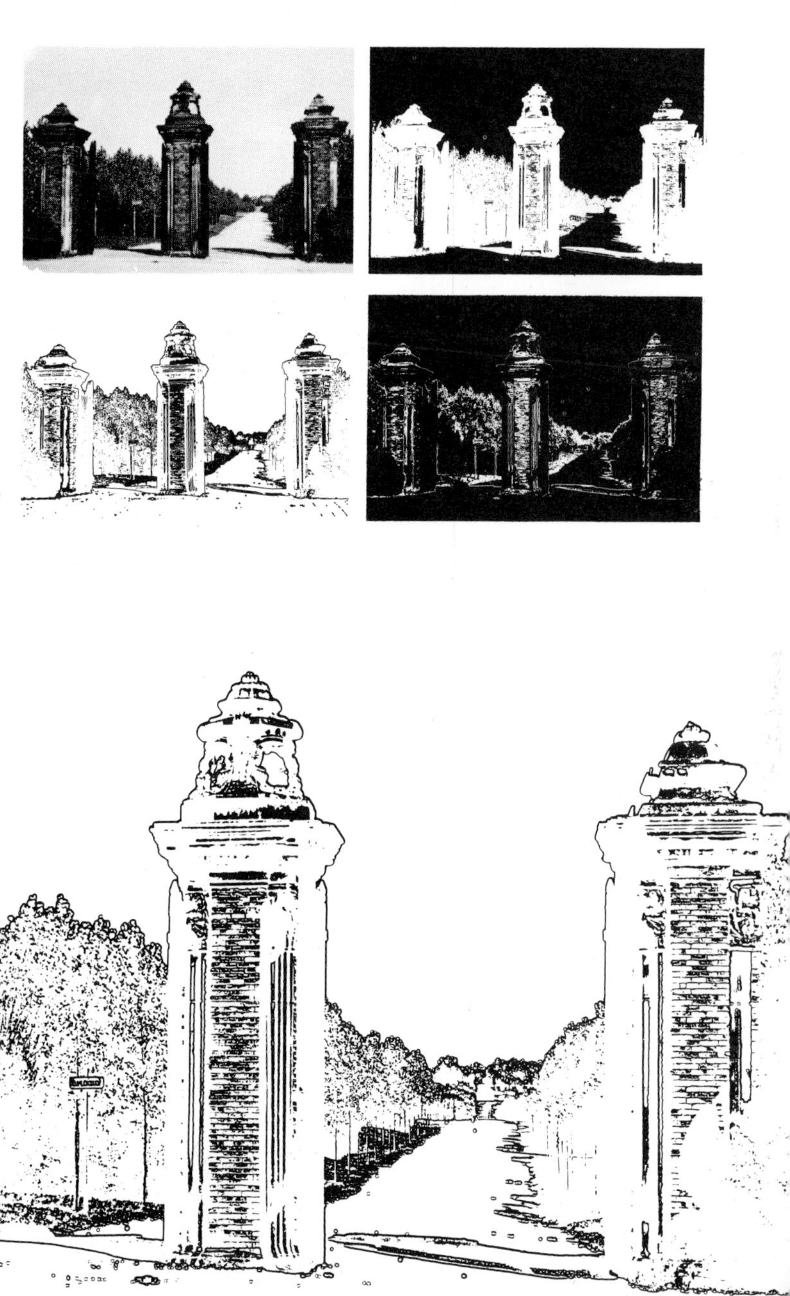

stage again in order to get a positive print.

As I mentioned earlier, an angle of 45° is usually about right for this process. The greater the vertical angle the thinner the lines. When the angle is less than 45°, the lines disappear.

If you place the negative and positive in register, close examination will show that in fact there is still a fine line showing between the image boundaries. Therefore a print made from this sandwich even in direct light will produce a line effect, as the illustrations show.

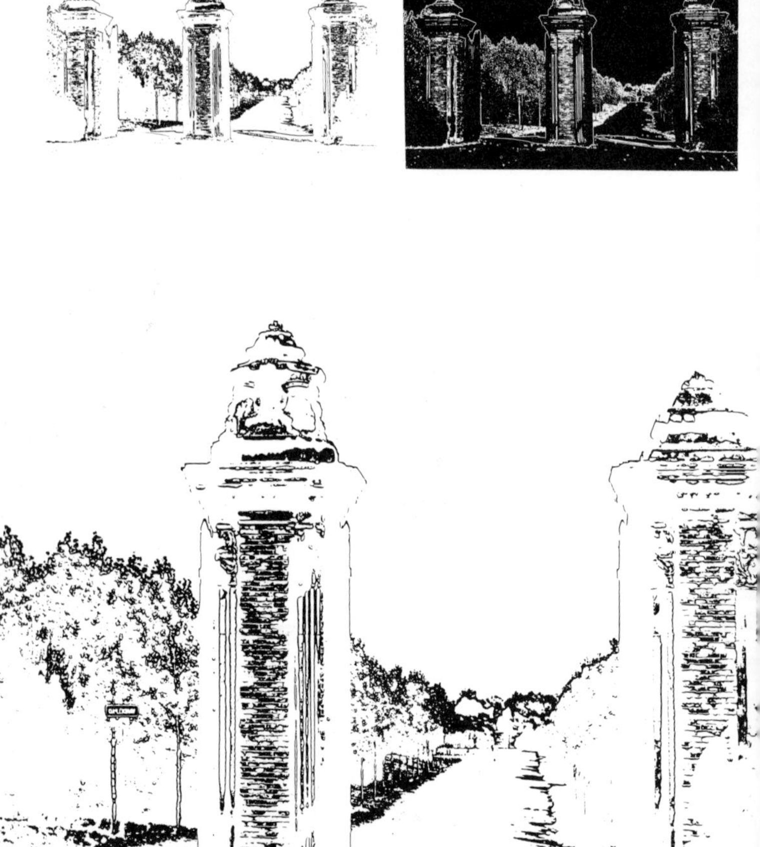

8. Derivations in colour

Each time anyone asks me what I think of derivations in colour, the first word that springs to my lips is "amazing". At the same time, that word sometimes carries an implicit condemnation and so I must add that most of the things I have seen that were really remarkable were also in colour.
Alas, I am past the time of life when I can appreciate a lot of random colours stuck next to one another. I want to make sure that colours appear in my work at the places I want them so and not somewhere else! A border full of variegated flowers may look lovely to the eye but I'm afraid I have to see them in terms of usefulness to the work I have in hand.

The majority of derivatives in colour – and I include here the work of such leaders in the field as Eimo Gareis and Gerhard Graeb – have all the charm of a multi-coloured ball of wool!

Working with colour is always difficult and in derivation work even more so. Certainly, if you print a number of negatives one after the other with high-value filters, or combine a number of different monochrome negatives, then you will get a lot of colour. Whether your effort will have been worthwhile is another matter entirely. The objective should be to get the right amount of colour in exactly the right place.
I see no reason why the use of colour should cause any change in your attitude compared with that which you adopt for black-and-white work and yet some people seem to lose their sense of proportion when working in colour. To find the right colours is no easy task, of course. The great stumbling-block seems to be thinking in terms of complementary colours and this is not easy in itself. It depends to a great extent on your training, by which I mean training in the sense of learning by experience, of comparing results with intentions and analysing the reasons for failure.

In practice, photographics in colour generally comes to the same thing as tone separation, of which more in Chapter 9. You can, however, start from any negative in black-and-white or colour, or even from a positive if you like.

Method

Stage One: Make a normal diapositive from a negative and perforate both with registration holes.
In addition, from the same negative make another diapositive with a very short exposure.

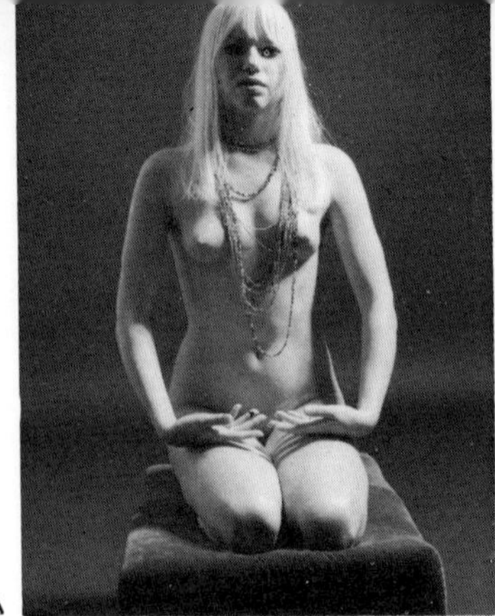

1A

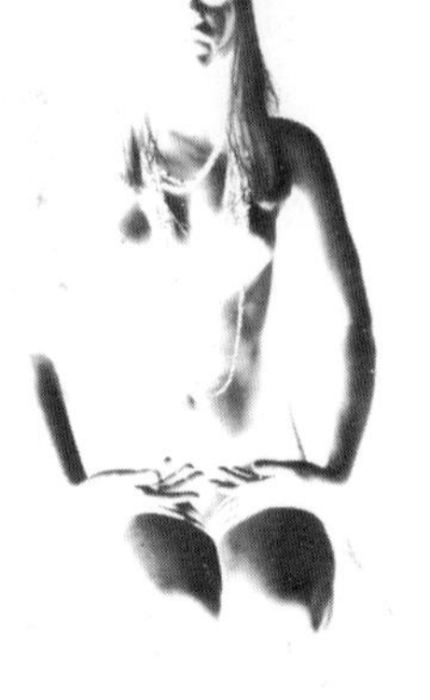

2A

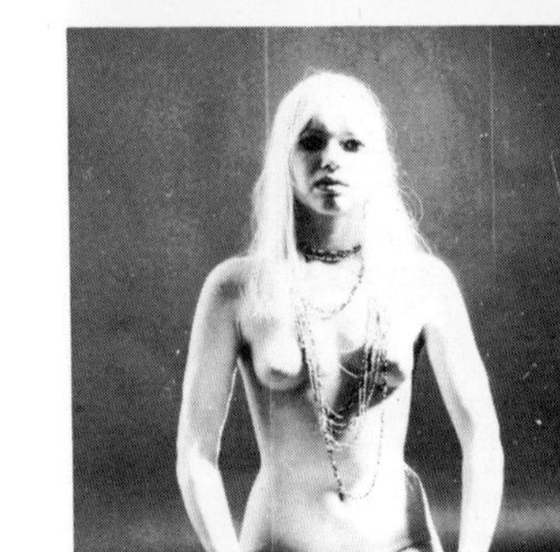

1B

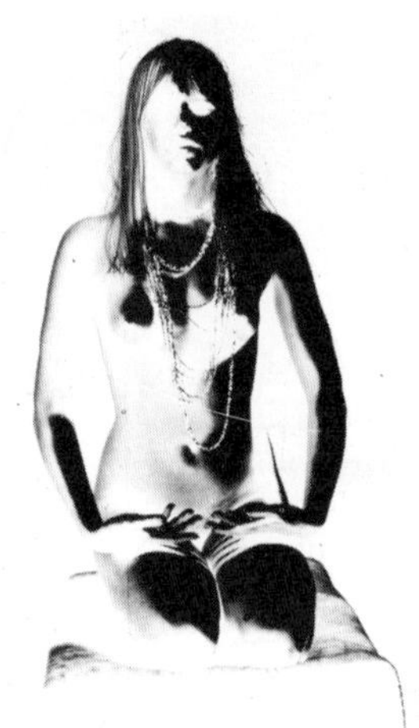

2A

2A

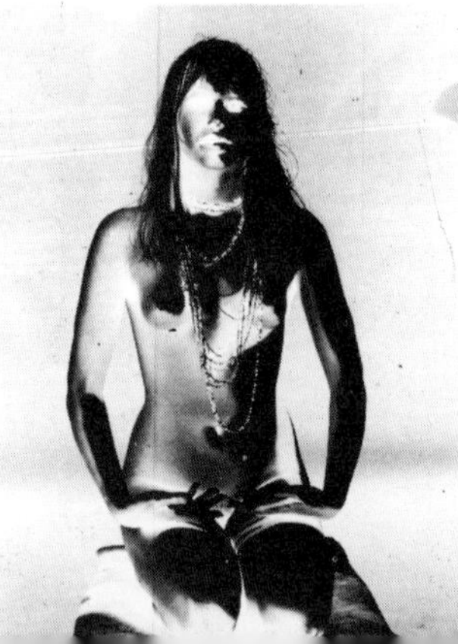

Stage Two: From the normally exposed diapositive, make three negatives with varying exposures. Then, using the underexposed diapositive, make a mask. You do this by giving it an exposure long enough to make the subject come out completely black and the background completely white, so far as possible. If there is any darkening of the background, bleach it out with Farmer solution and, at the same time, touch in any

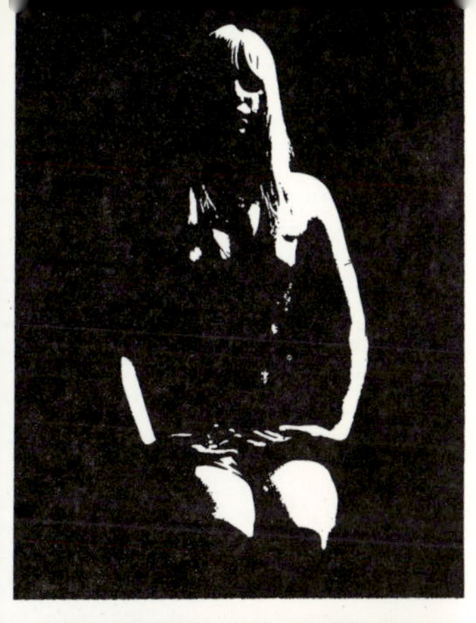

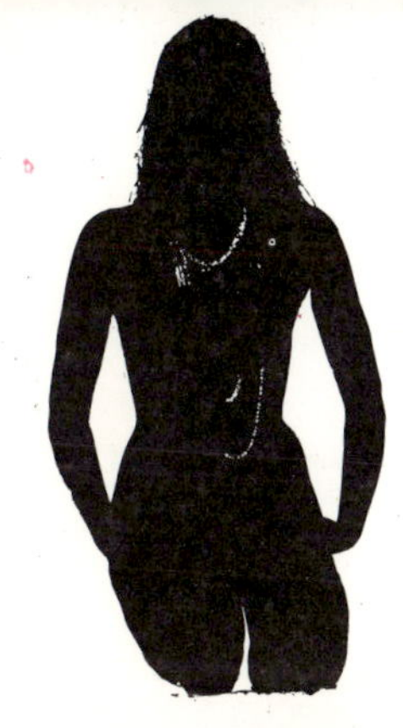

2B

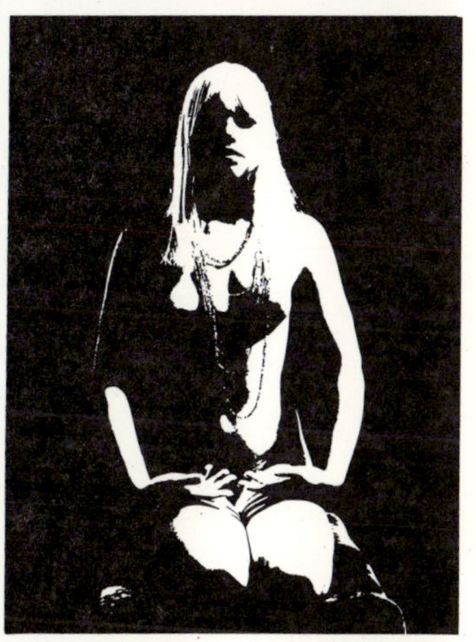

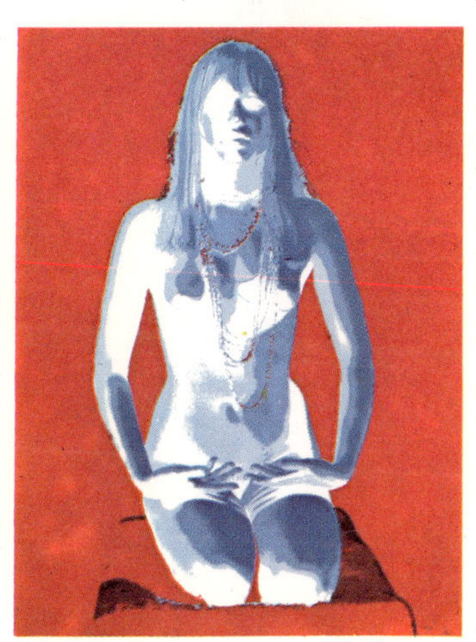

4

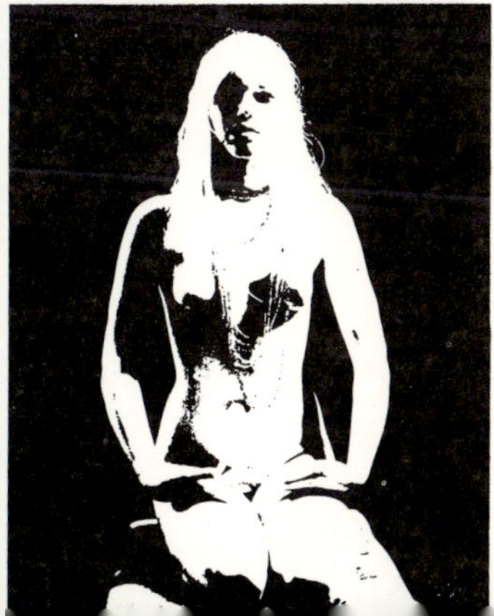

unwanted highlights that remain in the subject.

Stage Three: make three hard diapositives from the three negatives produced in Stage 2. We used O81 film in the examples.

Stage Four: All that remains now is to add the colour. Using Positive-M film, expose all three negatives in succession, using the perforations to keep them in register, through a set of filters giving 300: 100:-. After this,

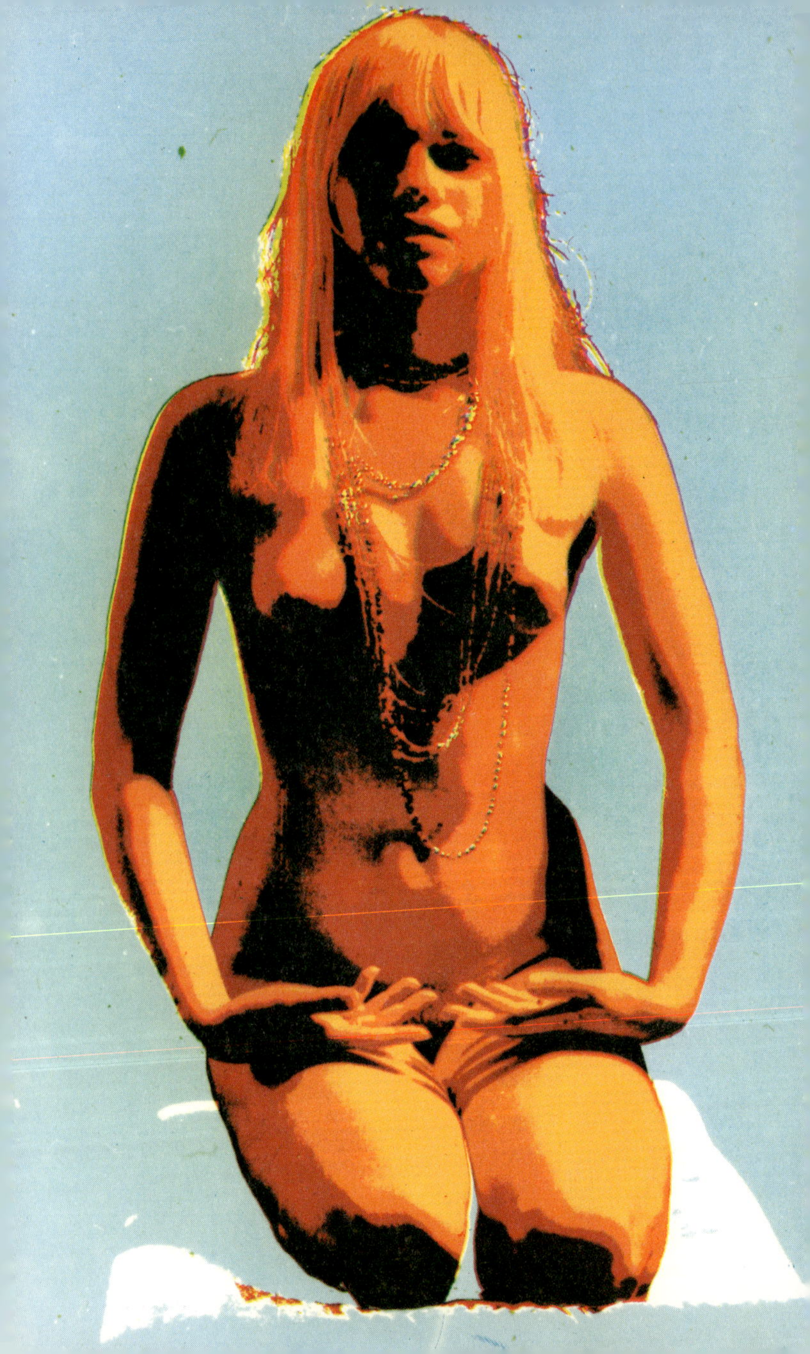

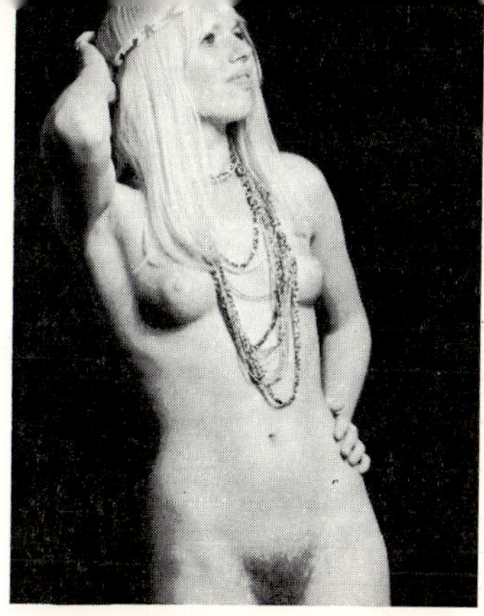

1

change the filter to 250:-:250 and expose the mask on to the same piece of film. The reproduction on p 50 is the result.

Solarization in colour

Stage One: Make a soft diapositive on N33p film or the equivalent (see Appendix).

Stage Two: Print on to Positive-M film, using 100:-:- for the first exposure and 300:-:200 for the second.

Stage Three: Print on to Positive-M film, with neutral filtration for the first exposure, and -:200:- for the second.

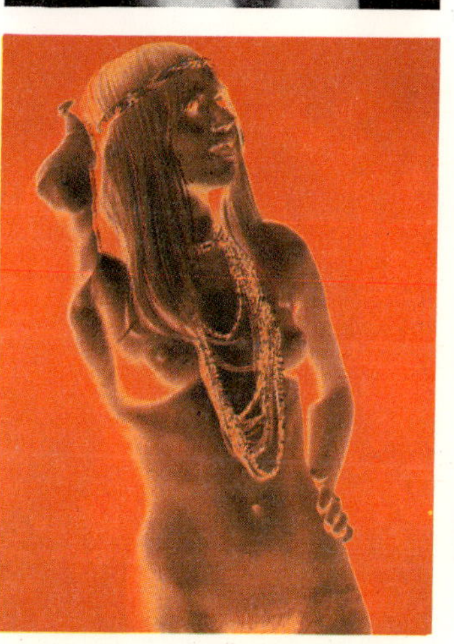

2

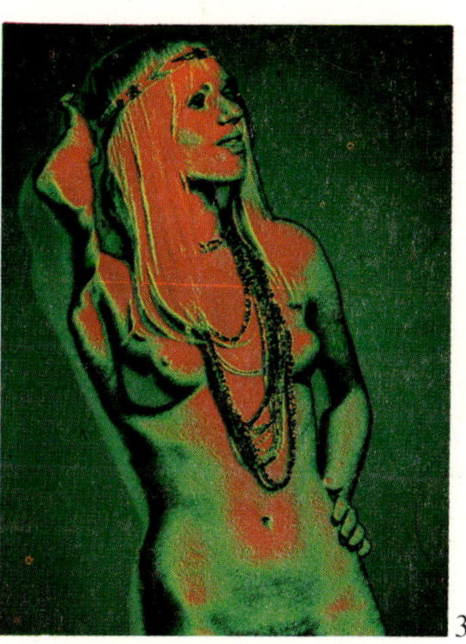

3

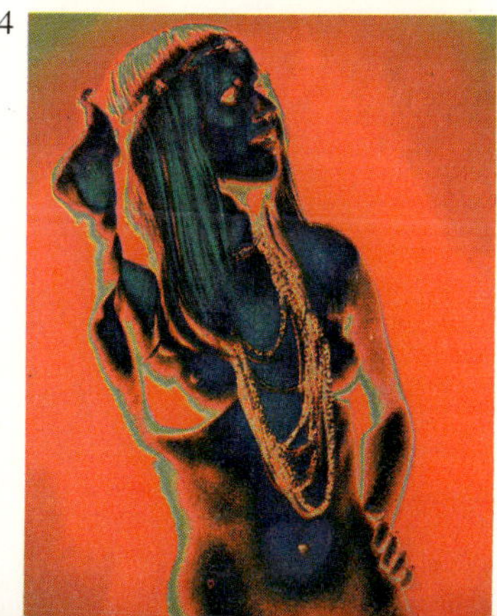

4

Stage Four: Print again on to Positive-M film, with neutral filtering for the first exposure and 300:-:- for the second.

If desired the process can be repeated. However, if the fourth stage is printed on to paper using filters set at -:-:100 the result should look like illustration on p 52.

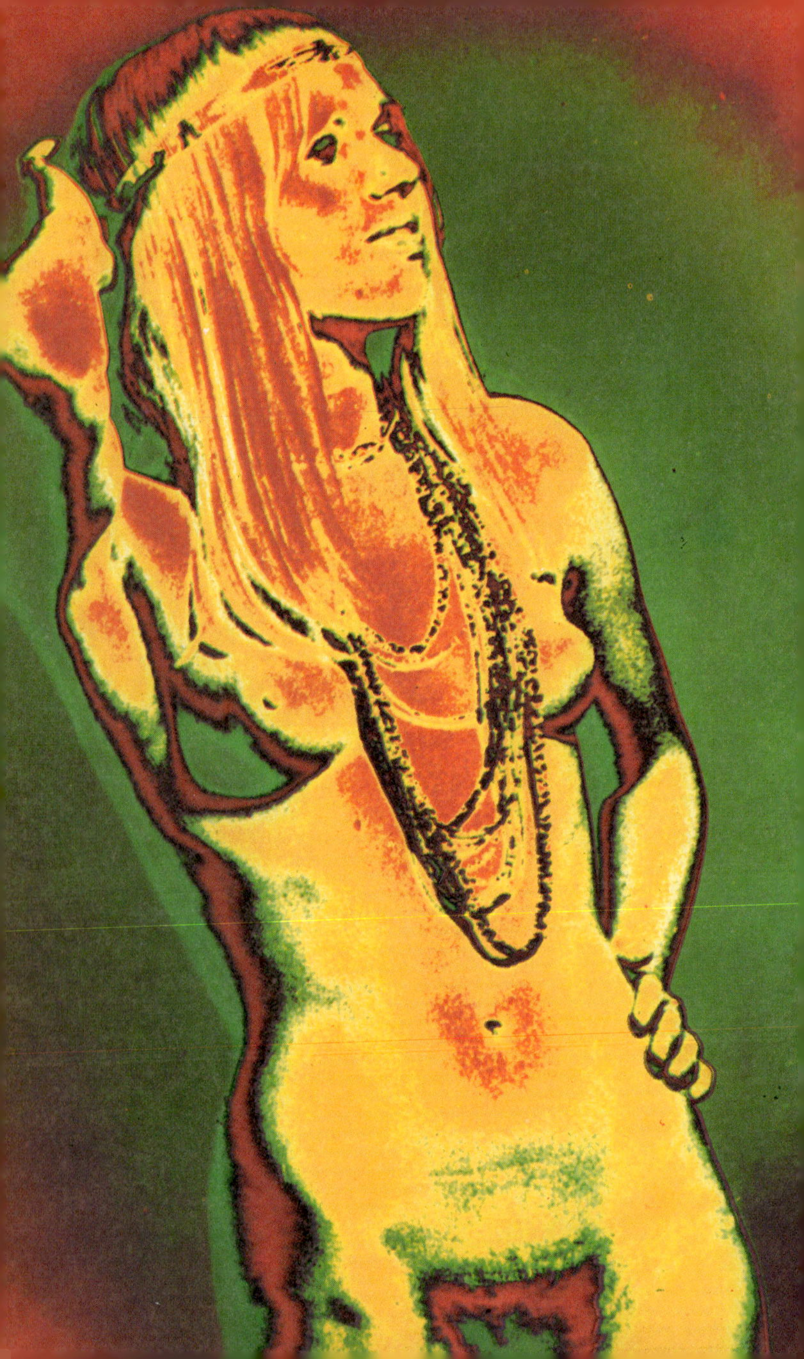

9. Tone separation

Isoheliograms

This is a technical term, but little used, for a half-tone photograph which has not been separated right down to lines and areas but where the range of tones has been severely reduced – to, say, only white, grey, and black. They are popularly known as "tone separations". You can have more tones, but five is the maximum because a sixth tone would be virtually indistinguishable.

There are various methods of doing this, all leading to very much the same result. However, the method given below has the advantage of being simple and, in addition, it needs no special apparatus and can be carried out after only a little experience.

The greatest problem is the grey tone. This can be obtained in one of two ways, the simpler one being to use a soft material such as Agfa N3lp or Kodak Commercial Ortho. When this is not available, you can manage by making a shorter exposure on to Agfa O8l or Kodak Ortho Royal material. This will, however, require an accurately-timed exposure.

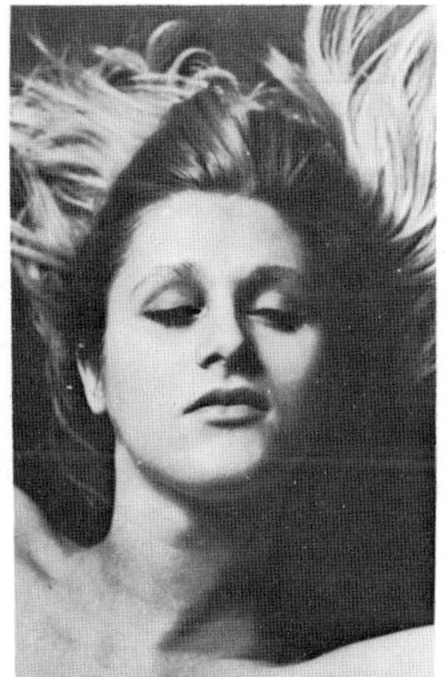

Method

Stage One: First of all make a reasonably dense but soft positive.

1st stage

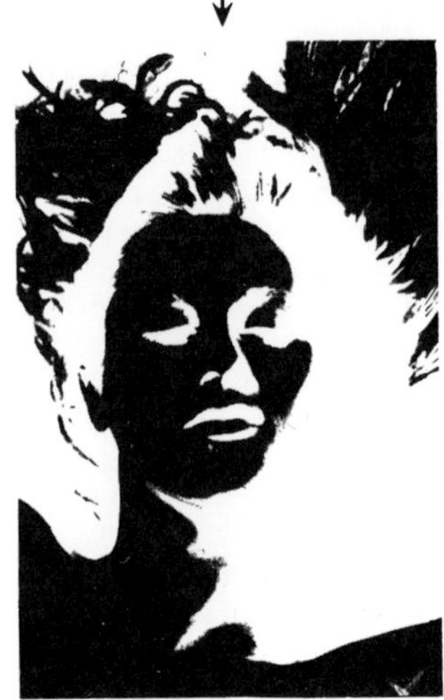

2nd stage A

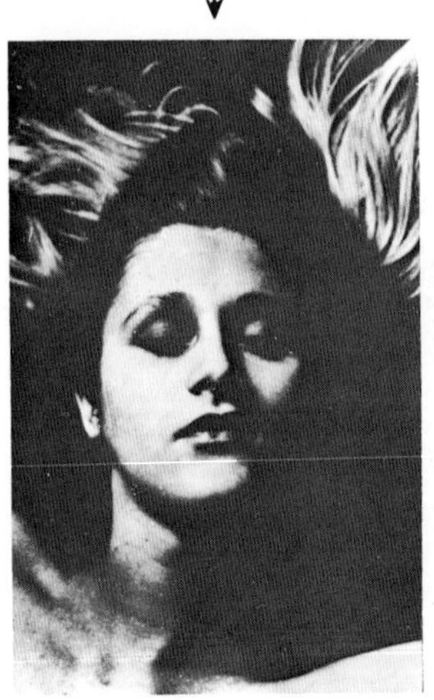

2nd stage B

3rd stage B

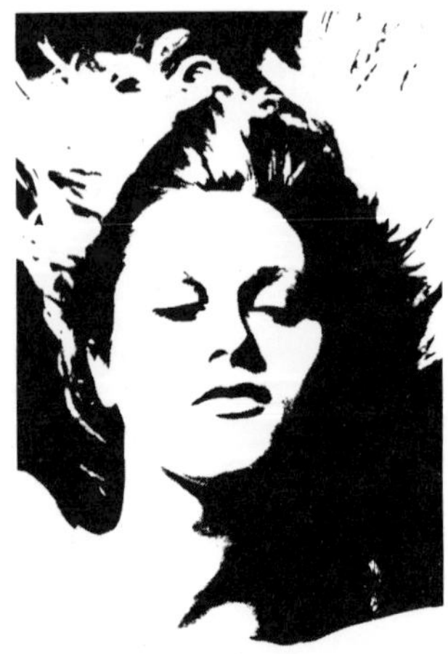

5th stage A

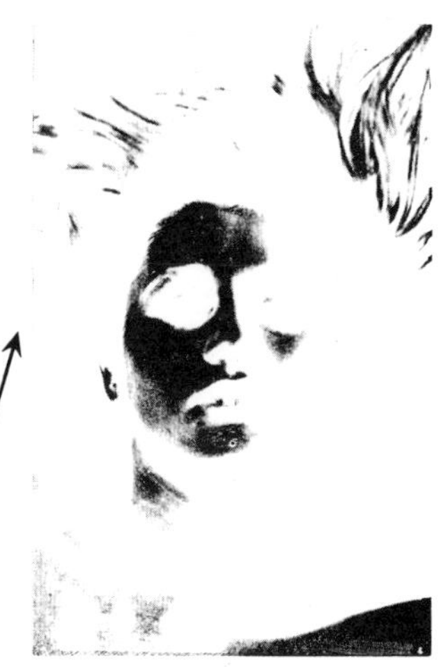

4th stage B

Stage Two: Using O81p or Kodak Ortho Royal make two negatives from this. The first one (A) should be exposed for a long time to get the black tone, and the other (B) should have shorter exposure for the grey.

Stage Three: Print (B) on to O8lp or Ortho Royal film.

Stage Four: The third stage is copied again to produce a negative with black and white areas *only*.

Stage Five: Positive from second stage A on O81 or Ortho Royal and positive from fourth stage on to N31 or Commercial Ortho. Then, register both positives, one on top of the other and copy on to negative material to get the result shown on p 56.

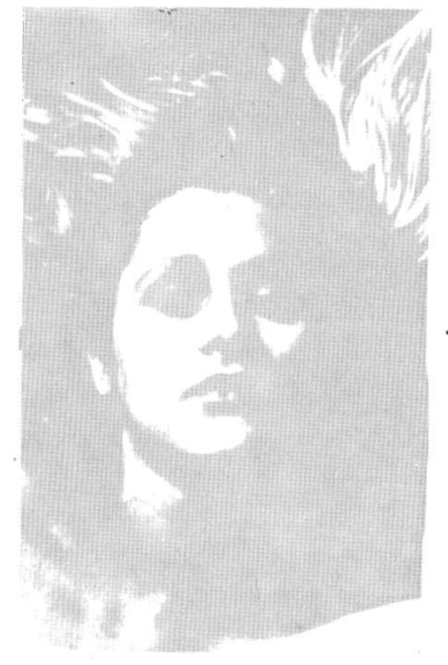

5th stage B

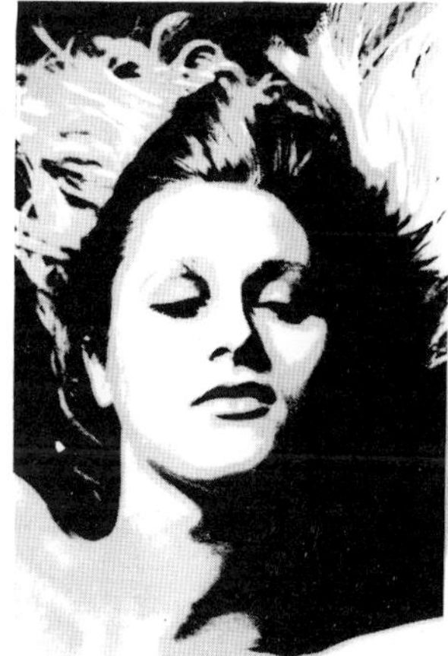

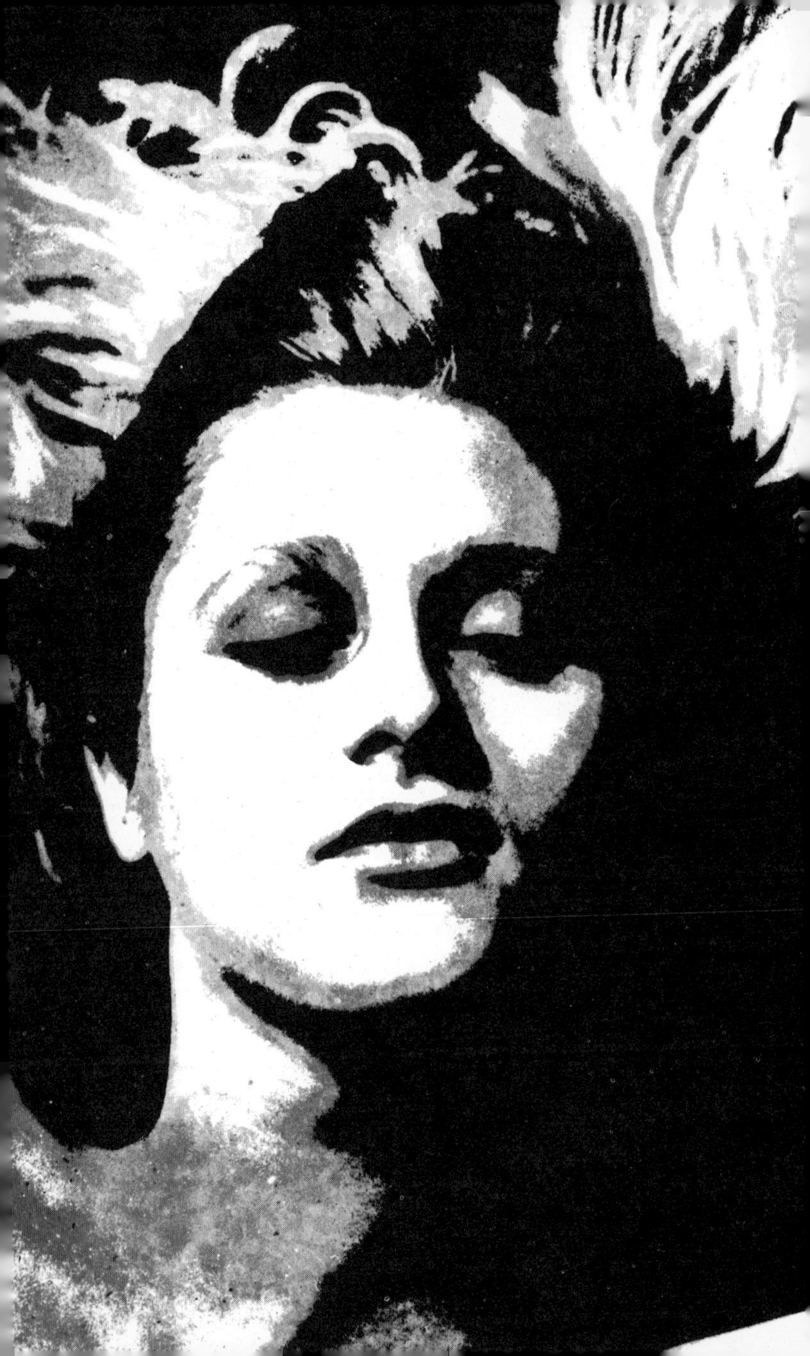

Tone separation using screens

The greatest difficulty with the process as described above is the grey tone. However, there is another difficulty, namely the lack of line in the image. This can be avoided by using the following method.

Method

Work as far as stage 4 exactly as previously described. You then make two negatives. On negative B you superimpose what is normally called a cross lined screen. These are available in most good photographic shops. What we have used here is a 60-60 screen – that is to say, one which has 60 lines to the inch and which covers 60% of the surface.

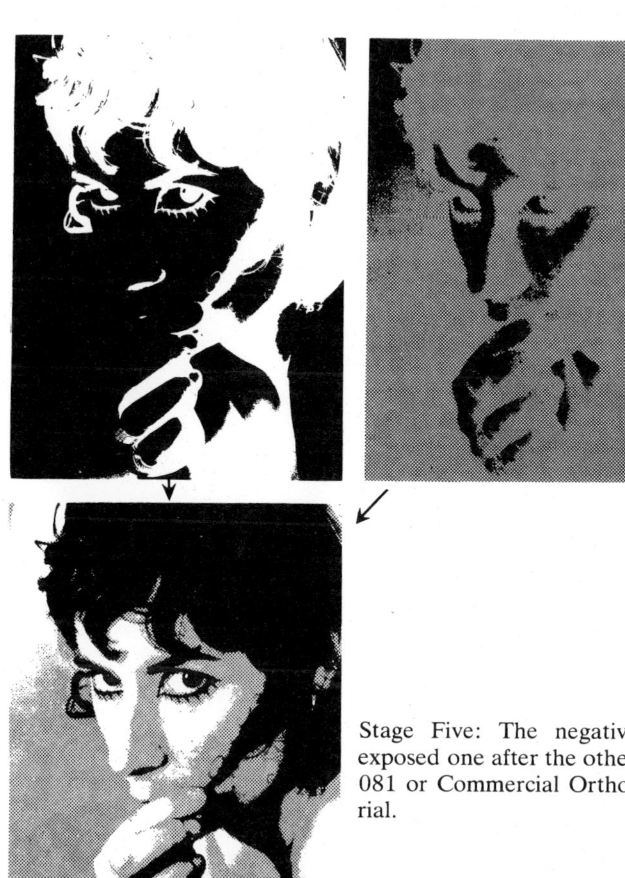

Stage Five: The negatives are exposed one after the other on to 081 or Commercial Ortho material.

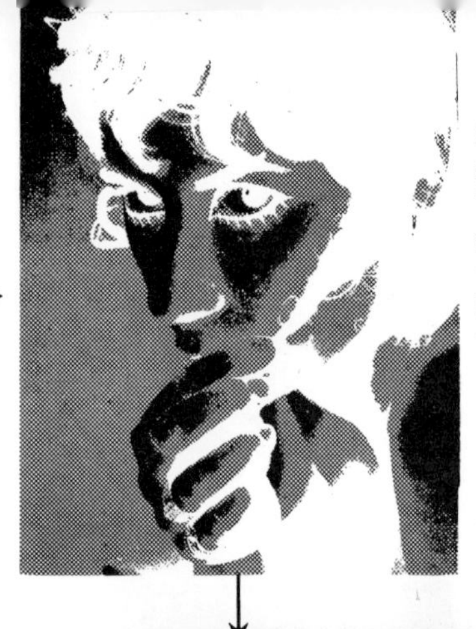

Stage Six: A further negative is made from this positive.
The "white" areas may not be completely clear in which case a weak bath of Farmers reducer can be used. A print of the final negative is given below.

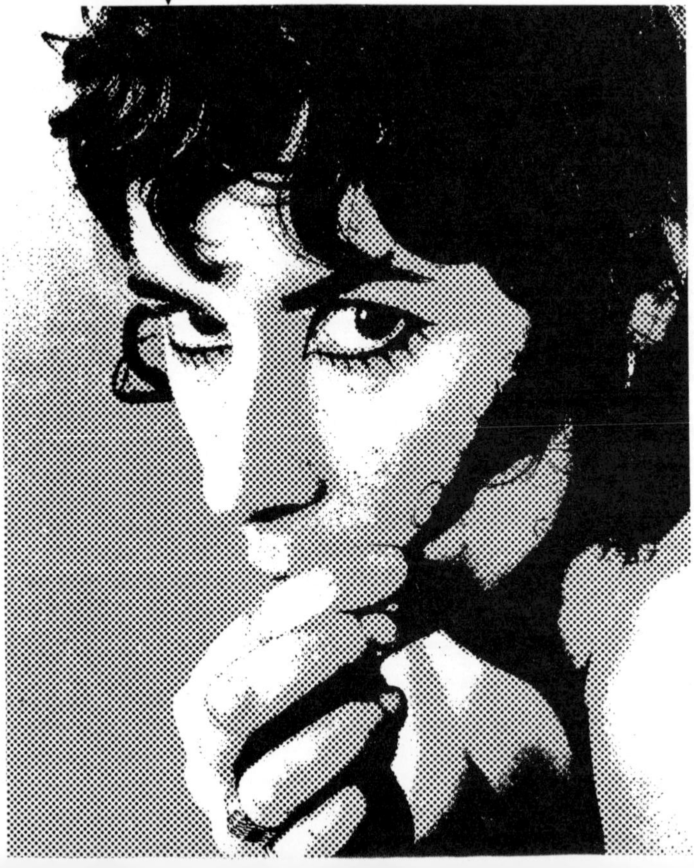

10. Combination Printing

Double prints

There are really two ways of producing double prints. The first is a double exposure from two negatives which are successively printed on to the same piece of paper. The second is only usable if the negatives have approximately the same density in which case they can be put together in the same holder and printed simultaneously, thus saving time over the first method.

Method

Stage One: Make a photogram of a piece of net using Kodalith film.

Stage Two: Put the negative of the picture you want to print into the enlarger and set it up slightly out of focus. Expose this on to a piece of photographic paper.

Stage Three: Mark the paper for register and remove it. Replace the picture negative with the negative of the piece of net. Focus this sharply, replace the paper, and print for maximum density.

The result of this sort of exercise is shown on p 60. I could, of course, have set both negatives up in sharp focus but then I would have lost the impression of depth that this photograph gives.

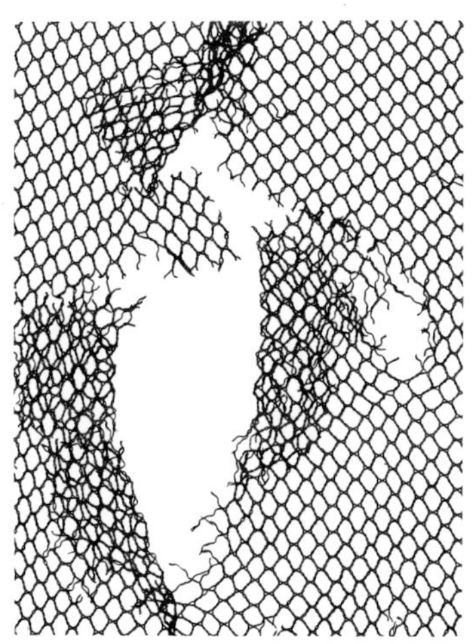

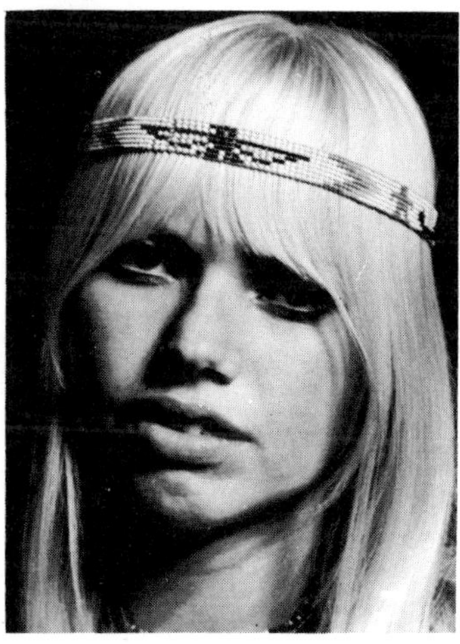

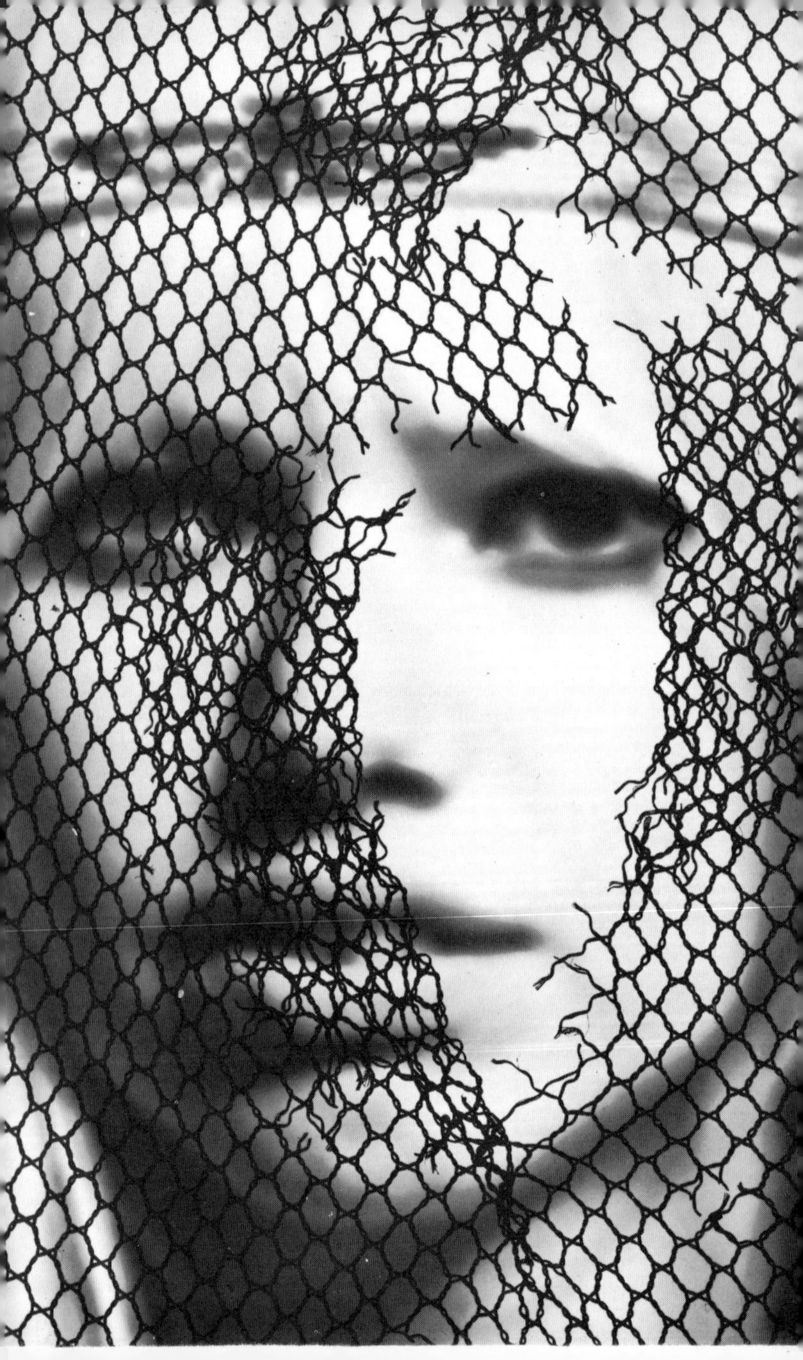

Montage

This is a process that I use a great deal. It is very versatile in that it enables you to bring people, objects and landscapes together in one photograph, and it allows you to build up your scene almost at will. In this way you can make shots which would otherwise be impossible. However, it is a process that requires great care and one that needs thinking about even when taking the initial photographs. The matter of perspective should always be borne in mind and you must be equally careful of camera heights and levels so that they are consistent.

Method

From the start, all films must be perforated for register.

Stage One: make a hard diapositive of the photo of the girl.

Stage Two: make a negative of this.

Stage Three: make a mask from the first stage. You do this by covering the whole figure in stage one with retouching paint, make a print on O81p, and then reprint to get a masking negative.

First stage: make a hard diapositive on O81 or Kodalith film.

Second stage: make a negative of this.

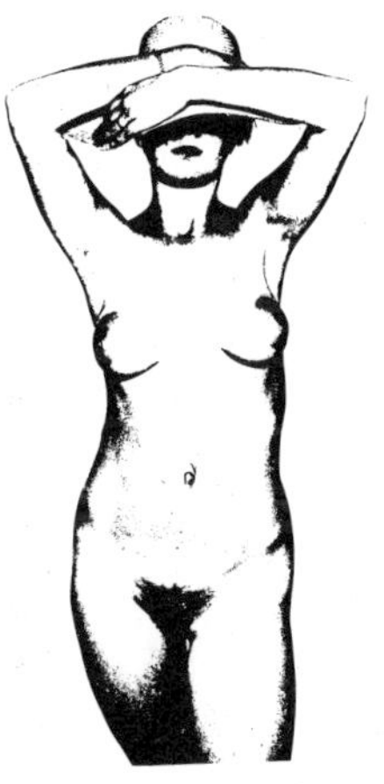

1A

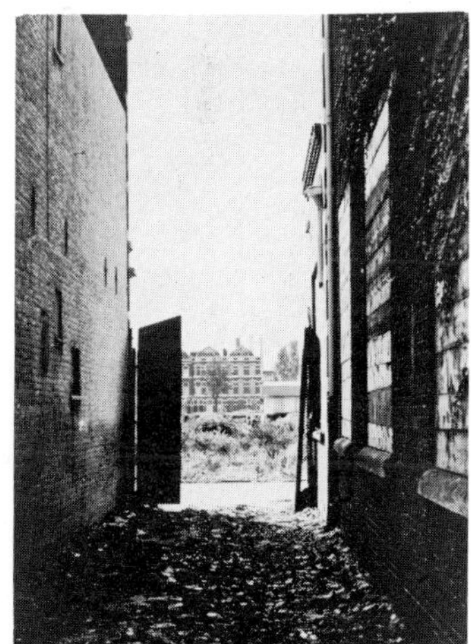

1B

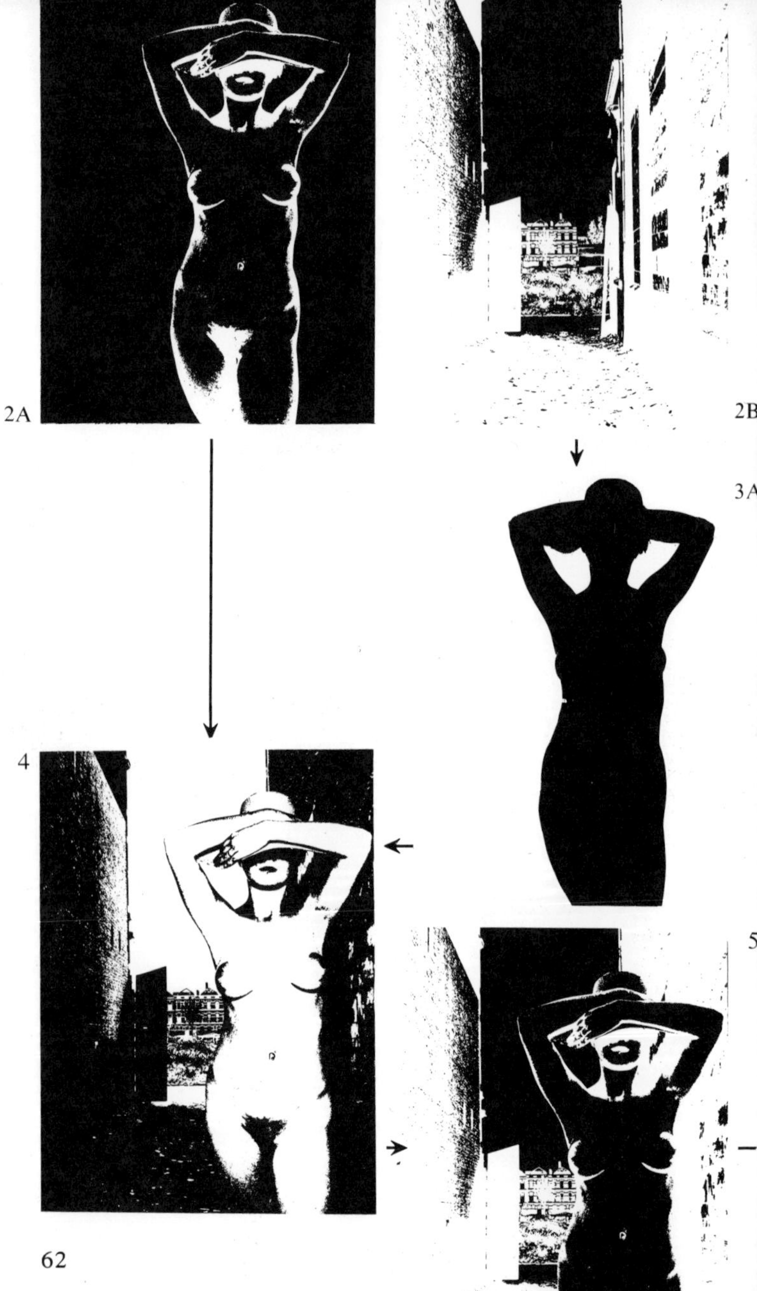
2A
2B
3A
4
5

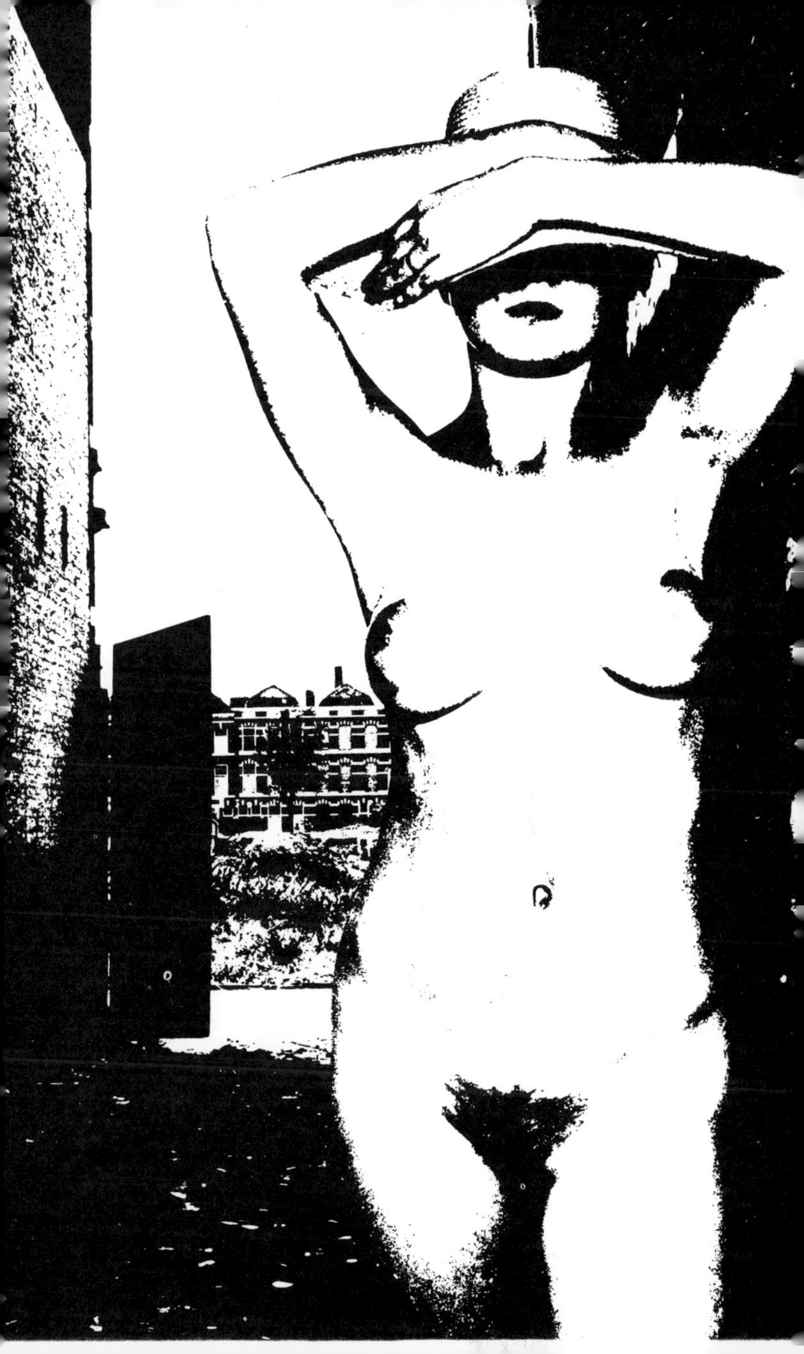

Stage Four: using the same material, you then expose on to it the negative of the second stage and the masking negative, one after the other. Afterwards, print the negative of the girl from the second stage without the mask.

Stage Five: make a negative of the fourth stage and then make a positive print from it.

You can print various negatives one on top of the other in this way.

You can also combine a grey and a black by printing them on the same sheet of paper but using different exposure times.

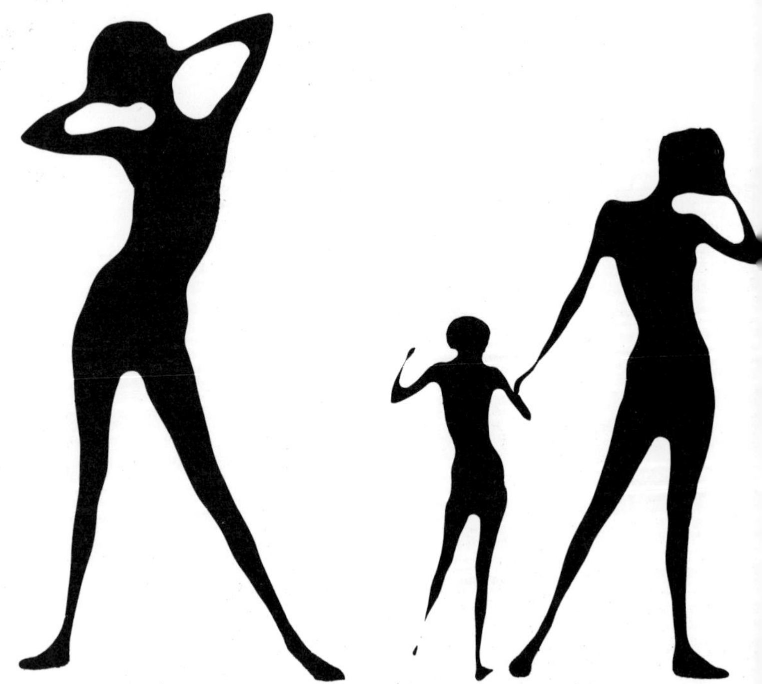

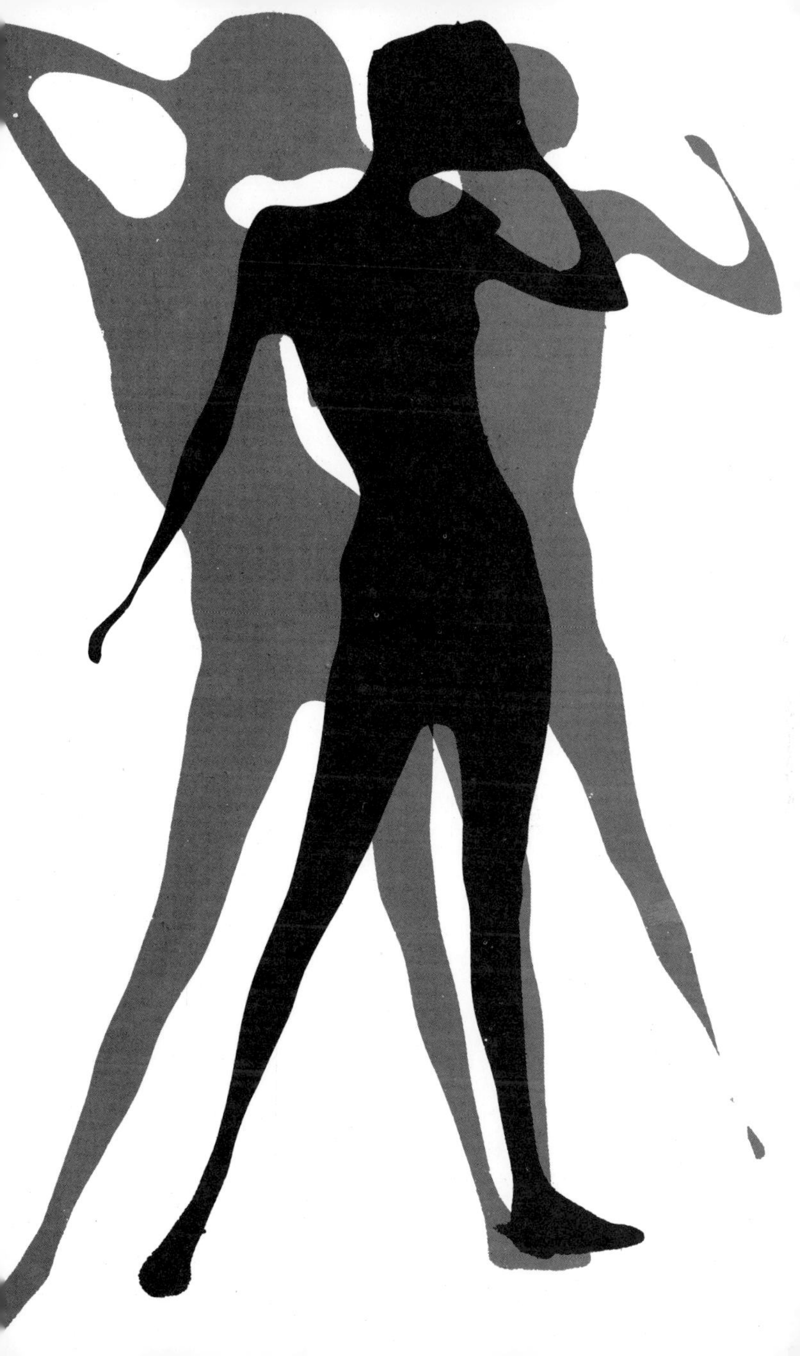

11. Screens

Texture screens, as they are usually called, are sheets of transparent material overprinted with a pattern and, as the name implies, they are used to add texture to a photograph. They come in a large variety of surface patterns nowadays and some have an adhesive layer but they are not as suitable for our purposes as those without this extra feature. Some makes have a darker overprinting than others and they are more convenient in that they need short exposures. In addition, the adhesive layer can also appear on the photo, which is why I recommend you not to use this type.
All you do is to lay the screen on top of the paper while printing and, depending on the exposure you choose, the pattern will be superimposed in either grey or black.

Method
After removing the intermediate tones by recopying as described in previous sections, cut a small piece of screen film, and lay it over the face during exposure. This will give a slight grey effect.

Do-it-yourself screens
While there are nowadays more screens available on the market than you could ever make yourself, it is cheaper to make them and you can get more variety. All you have to do is take some photographs of suitable surfaces using side lighting to bring out the texture but make sure it is even all over. The sort of surfaces you can try are tree bark, brickwork, woven mats, coarse cloth and so on. The only advice I would give you is not to let yourself get carried away with this sort of thing. A great deal of self-control is needed, because it is only a small step from using these screens successfully to being tempted to use them too much and on unsuitable subjects.
Another useful material for do-it-yourself texture screens is the

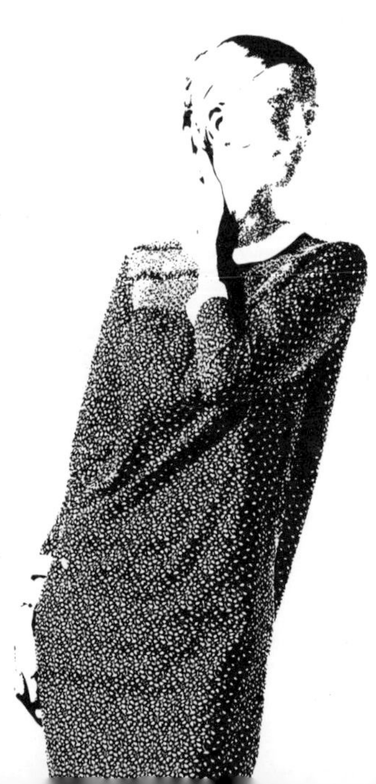

transparent plastic floor covering material that can be obtained in various lengths nowadays. When buying this you must check whether the pattern on it is impressed in relief because the lines of the pattern, if they are raised up in this way, can act as a lens.

Method

Stage One: From a soft negative, make an enlargement on to a soft material such as N33p. Overlay the paper with a piece of the plastic material, making sure that the centre of one of the circles lies exactly between the eyes if the subject is a close-up portrait.

Stage Two: Copy this on to O81p, choosing an exposure that will still allow the concentric circles of the pattern to be visible in the shadowed areas.

Stage Three: Recopy several times to remove the half-tones.

Stage Four: Make a negative at the end of stage three and then make a print.

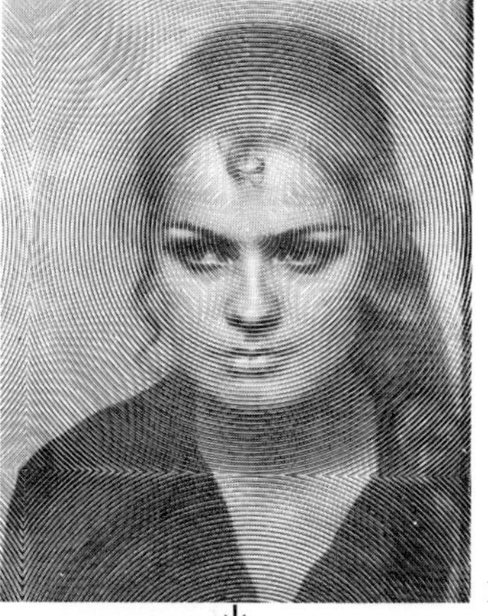

1

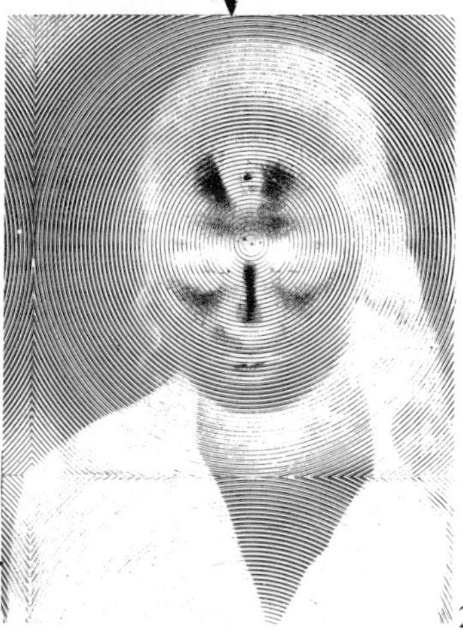

2

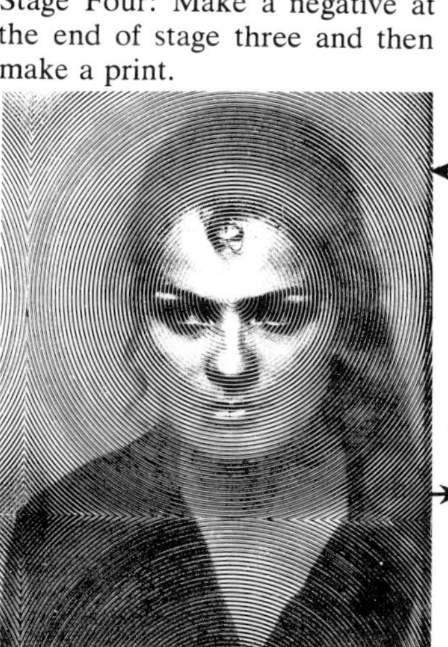

3

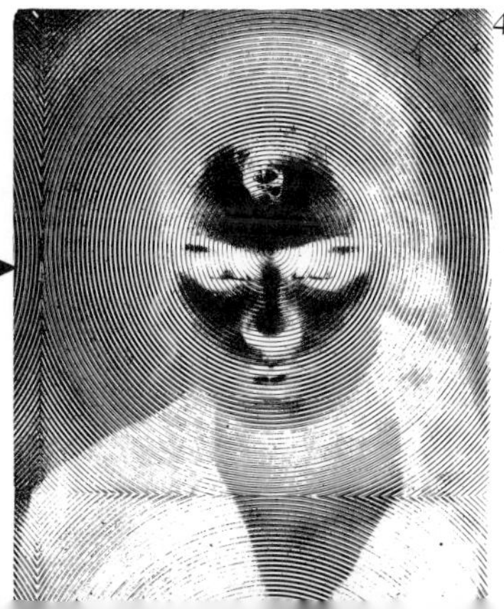

4

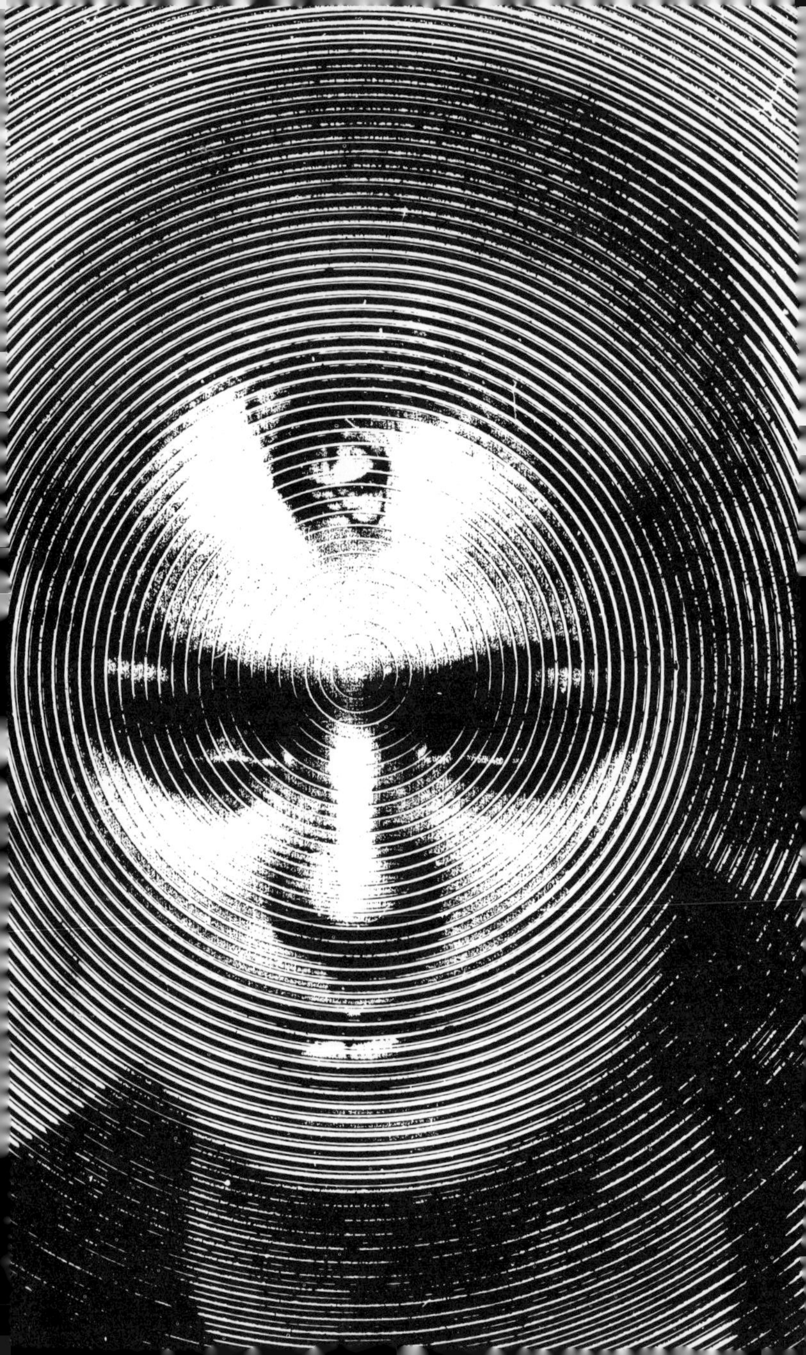

Graphic screens

The disadvantage of the type of screen we have been talking about is that the line pattern tends to disappear in the highlights. If you want to have an overall pattern that really is an overall pattern, then you have to take a leaf out of the photo-engraver's or platemaker's book and use a graticule screen.

They use a special screen, sometimes called a half tone screen that divides the picture up into a series of small diamond-shaped dots which lie closer together the darker the area of the photograph. However, these screens are very expensive and so I have developed a method of my own which gets the same sort of effect rather more cheaply.

I just use a simple line pattern, such as the one available from graphic industry suppliers (Proops of Edgware Road, London NW9). With this screen the spaces between the lines are the same width as the lines themselves. In order to keep the screen flat I lay it between two pieces of glass and then mount this sandwich *above* the piece of printing paper. The glass must be *absolutely* level, so check it out very carefully. You can support it on two pieces of wood but make sure that they are exactly the same height. You will have to determine the clearance for yourself by trial and error but it will most probably lie between 1 and 3 cm.

The actual clearance you will need is linked with the aperture you are using and the shadow of the lines on the print will be sharper the lower the glass sandwich, and the smaller the aperture.

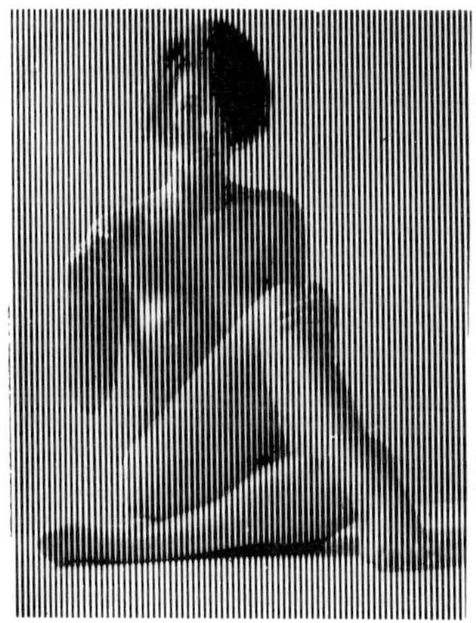

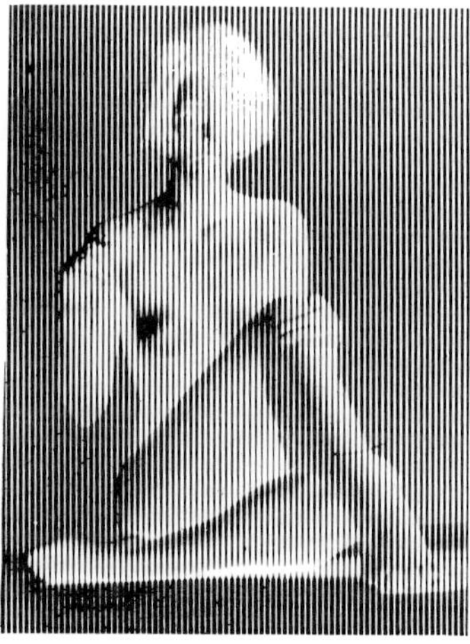

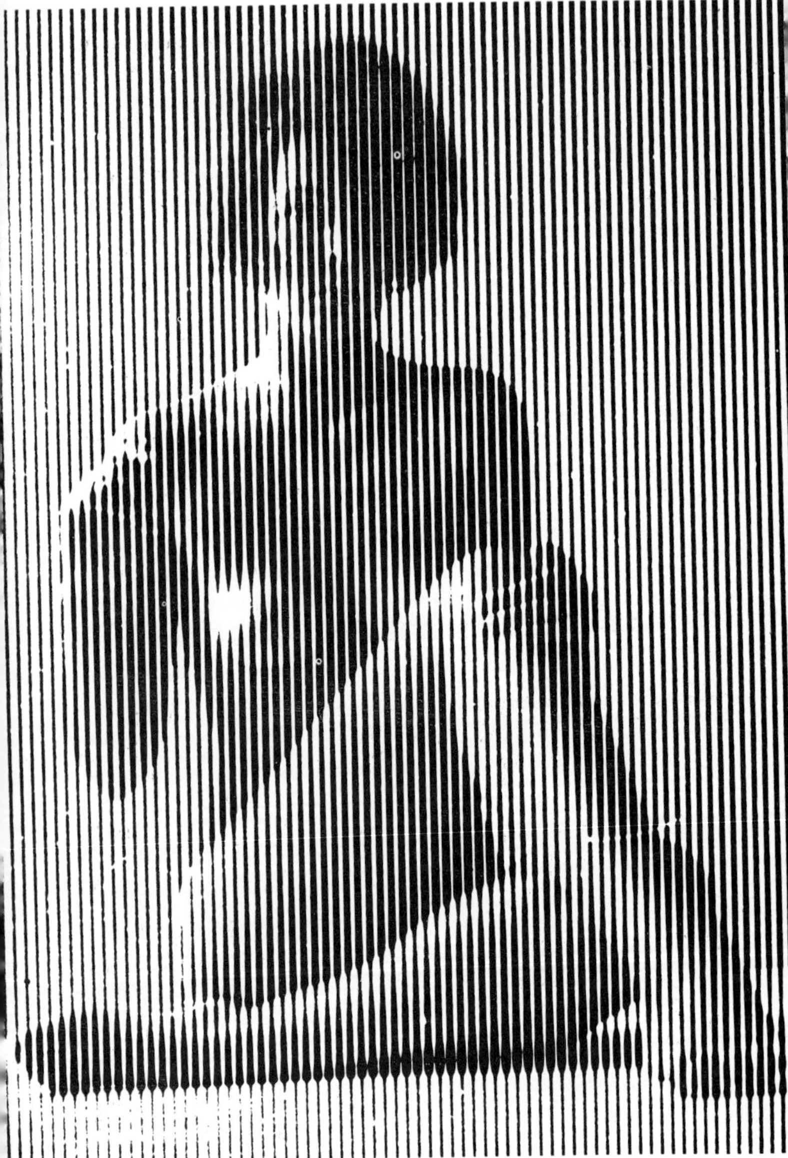

Method

Stage One: Make an enlargement of the negative on to O81p. For a trial make the height of the screen above the material 14 mm and use an aperture of f/16. You have to choose an exposure that will keep the lines visible in all parts of the image.

Stage Two: Copy this first stage on to O81p once again.

Now make a print from this negative. You will find that the lines are broader in the shadowed areas and thinner in the highlights, as the examples reproduced here show quite clearly.

Effect of aperture

The first exposure is critical. Where a lot of light passes through the material, a large part of the out-of-focus shadow of the screen line will come out as black. At the other extreme, a small amount of light passing through the material will cause the strip to be reproduced as a thinner line.

Since the shadow will be sharper (and hence blacker) at smaller apertures, it is possible to control the contrast directly by adjusting the aperture. Small apertures give blacker lines, while large apertures give thinner and greyer lines. As a comparison, the print on p 72 is the same as that on p 70, except that it was made using an aperture of f/11.

You can see from this that here we have a marvellous method of producing pictures to a tightly controlled specification. Whatever your taste, just set the aperture – wide for soft, small for hard – and the results will follow with precision.

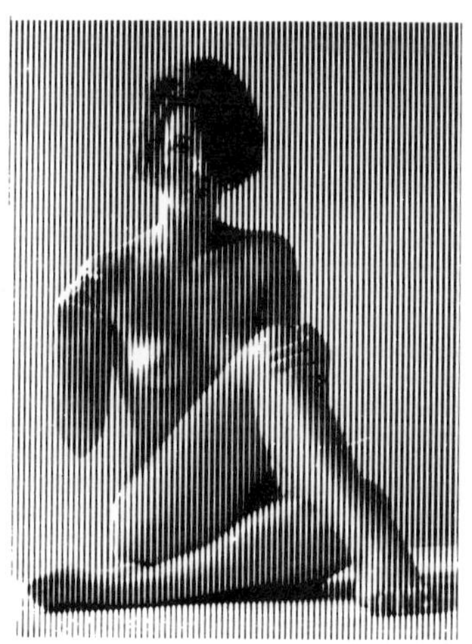

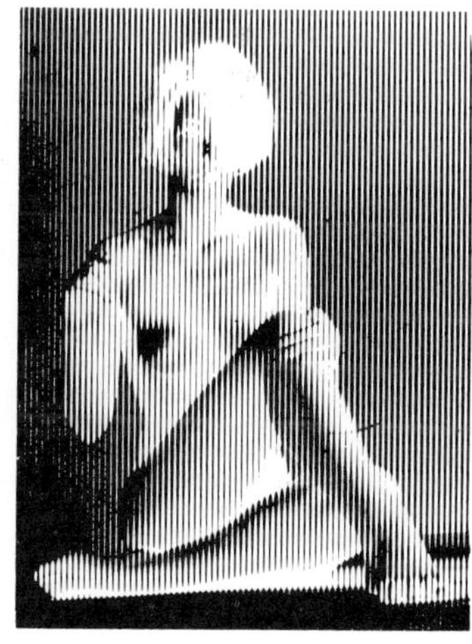

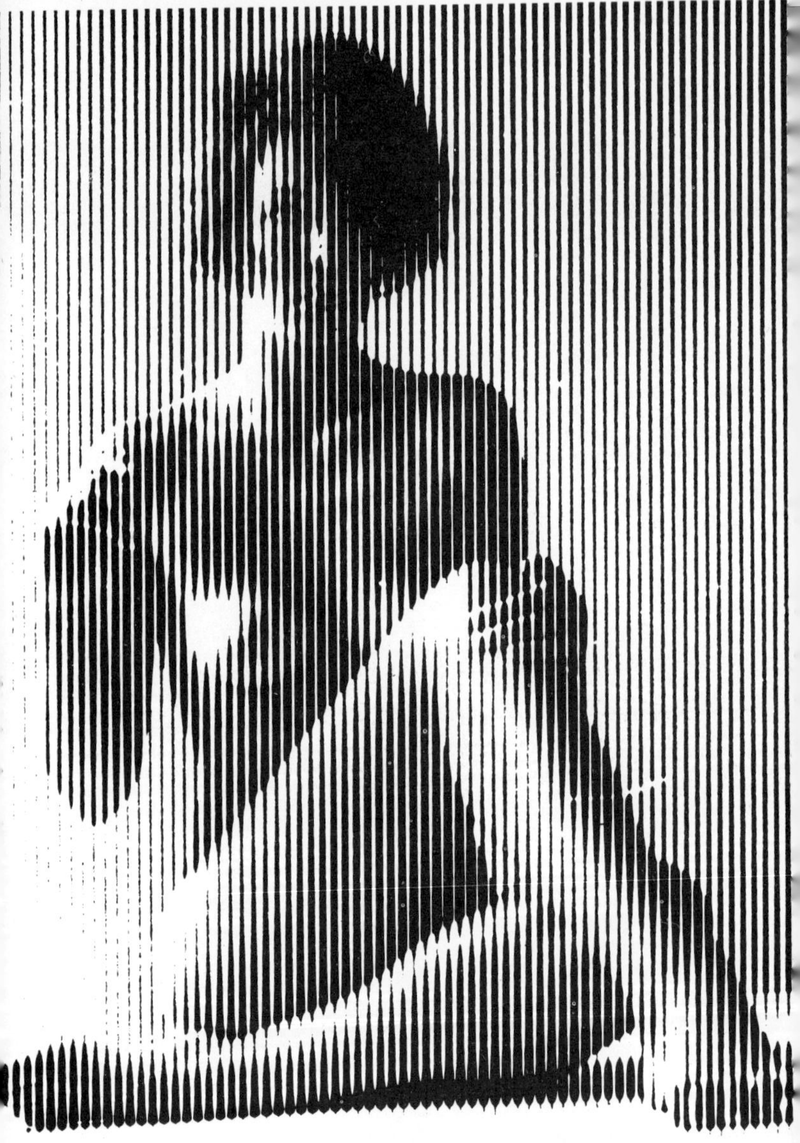

A step backwards

Sometimes the line will turn out a little too black and some modification will be necessary.

As the result reproduced below shows, this effect can be obtained by solarizing the second stage. However, this is something of a reverse step as far as control is concerned and so, perhaps, the tone-line procedure described in Chapter 7 is the best technique to use for this purpose.

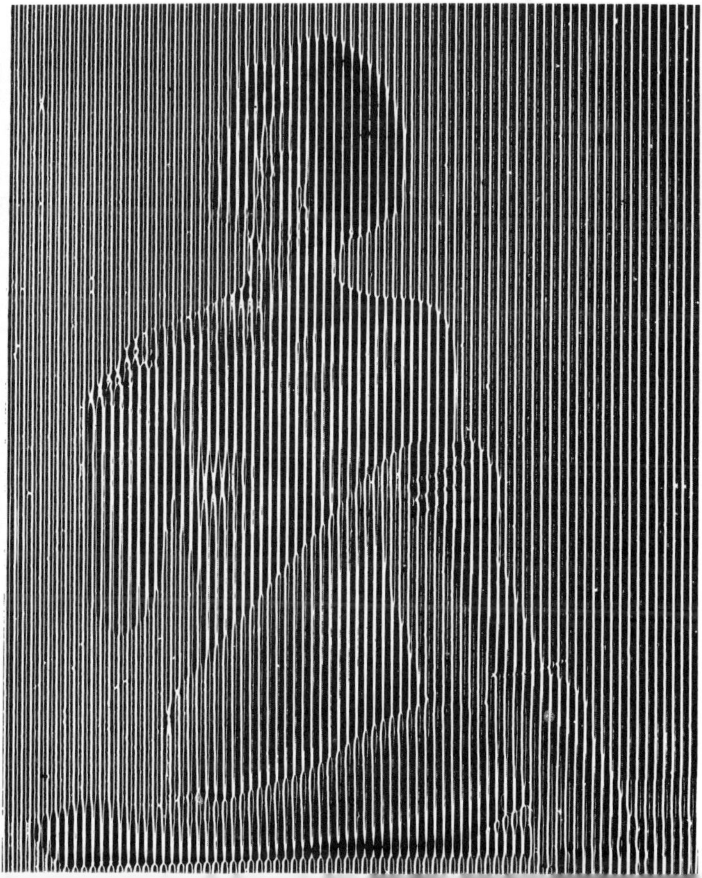

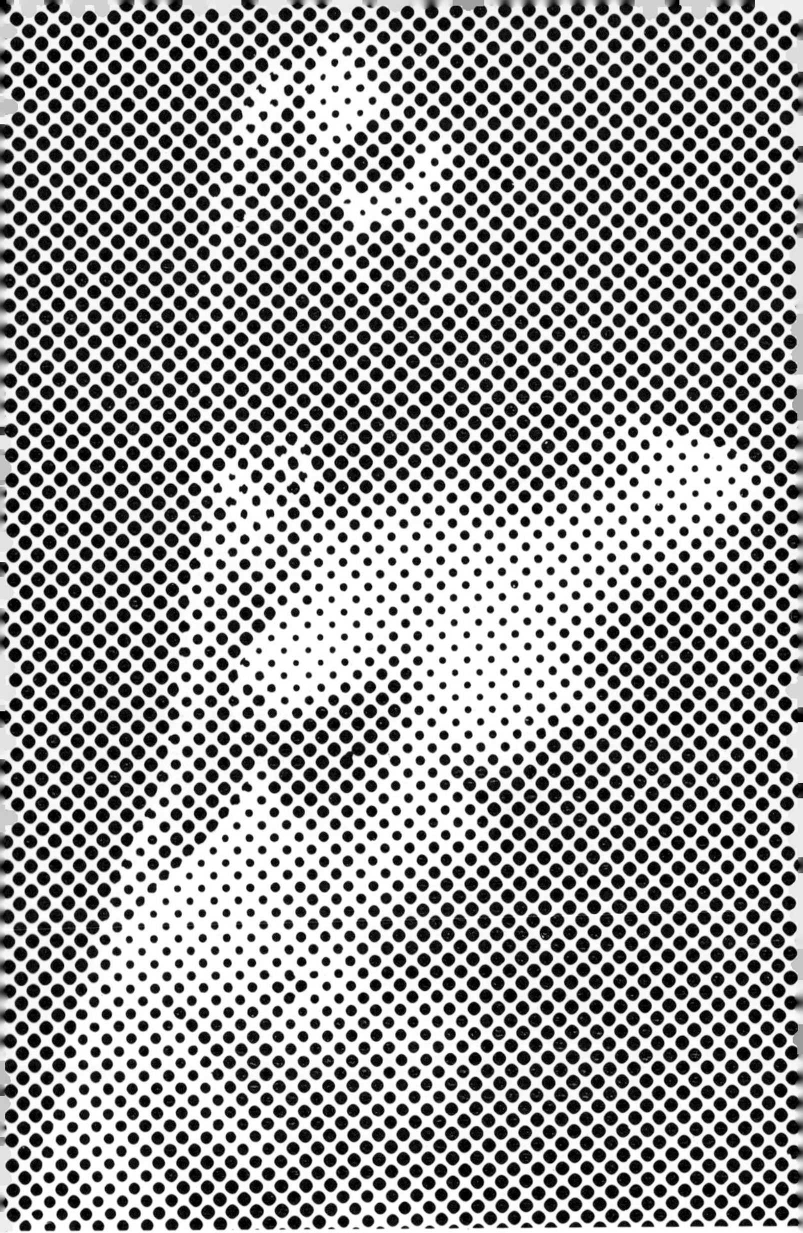

Of course, lines are not the only type of pattern that can be used in this way. These two examples show how a dotted screen can work in the same way with large dots in dark areas and small ones in highlights.

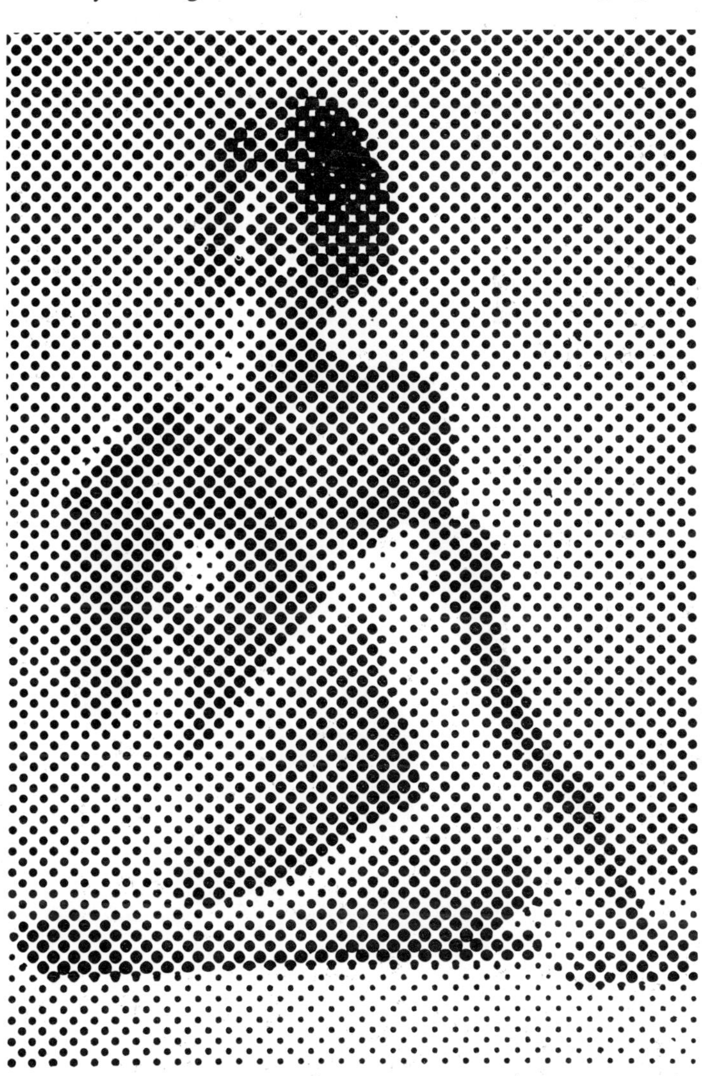

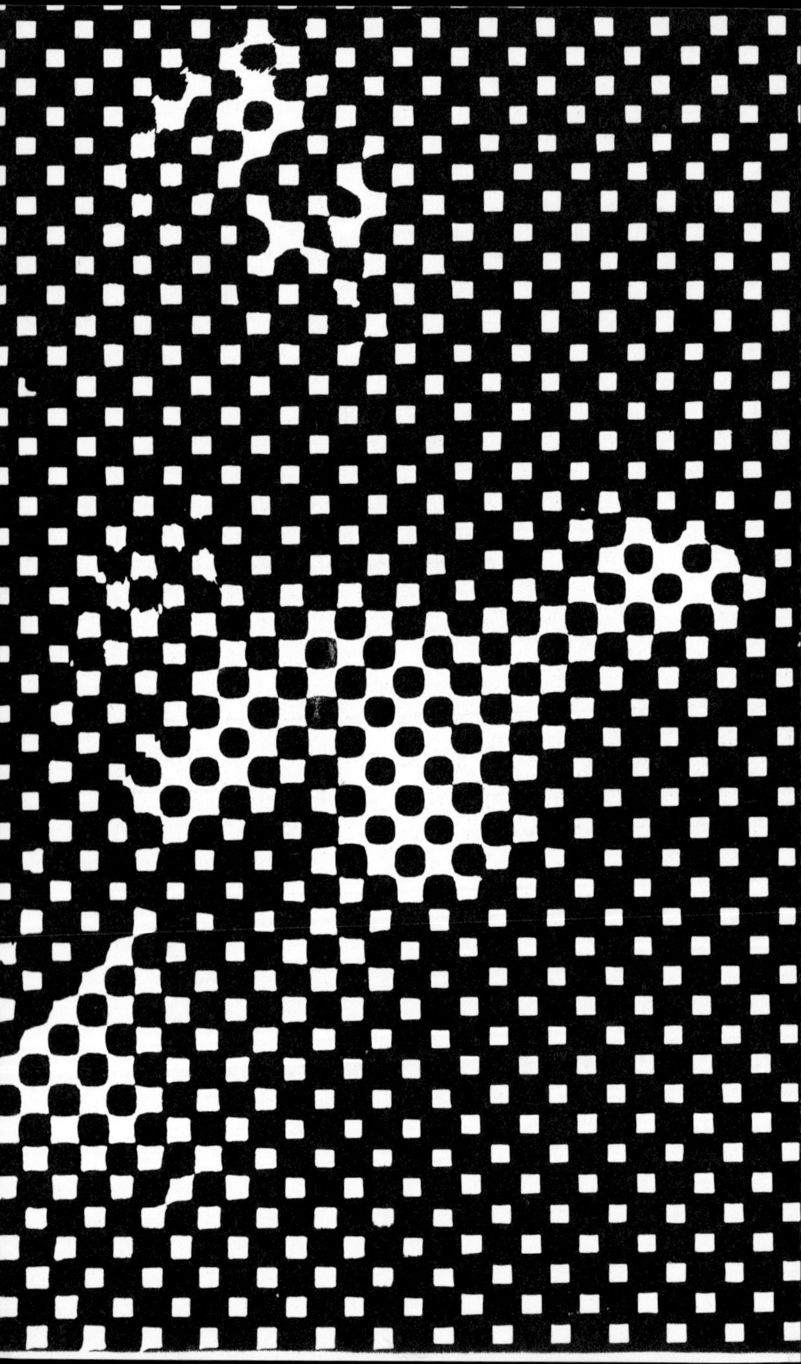

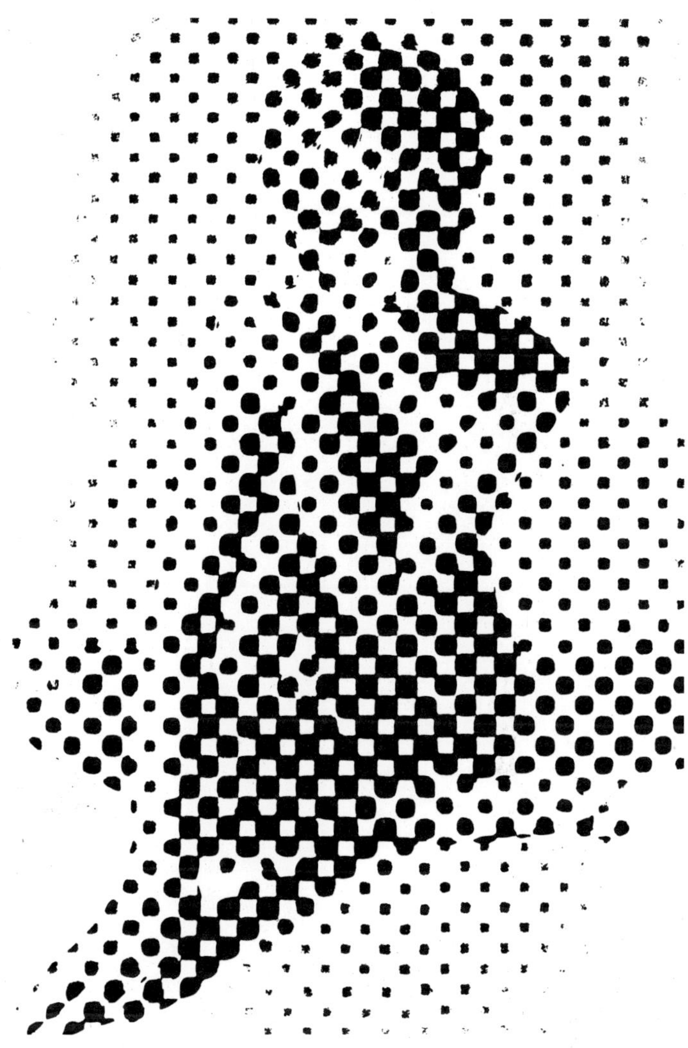

As the coarseness of the screen increases, so the recognition factor of the picture decreases, although the effect can sometimes still be striking.

Tone separation using screens

Method

Stage One:

a. Make a diapositive using a fairly long exposure with the screen in the "north-south" direction.
b. Make a second diapositive with about half the exposure of the first, and with the screen in the "east-west" direction, i.e. at right angles to the first.

Again, the material was 081p, and

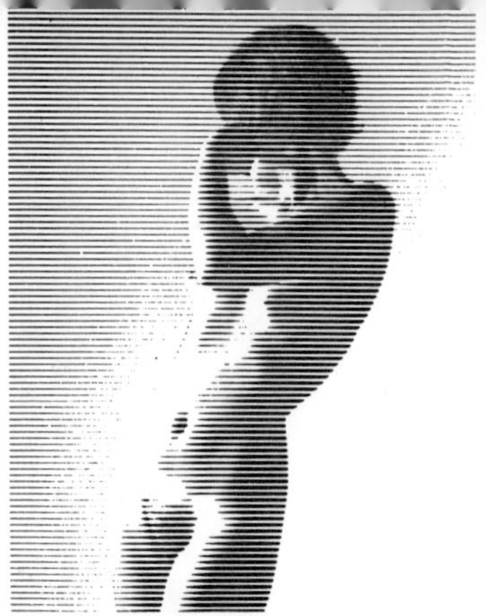

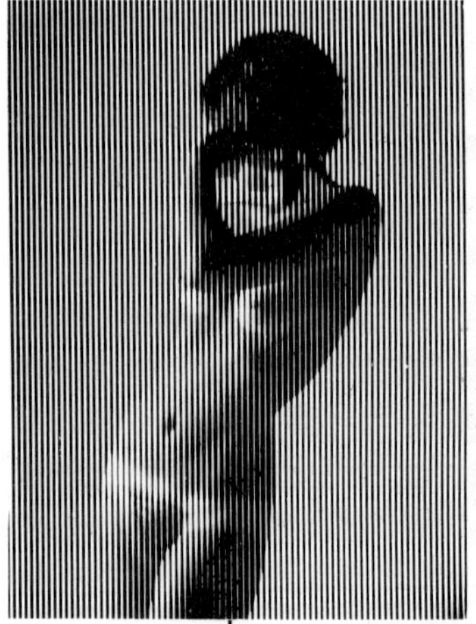

1a

2a

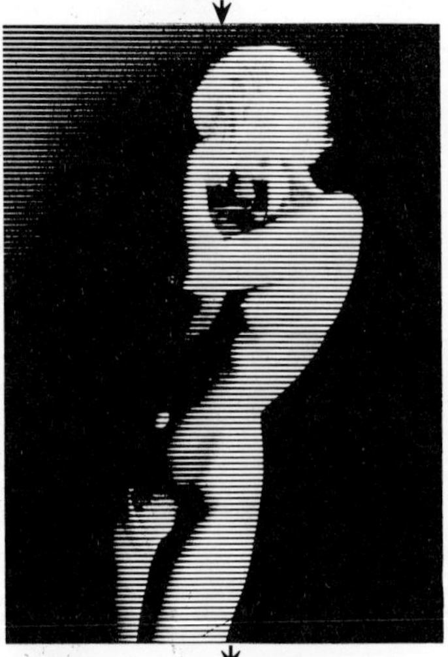

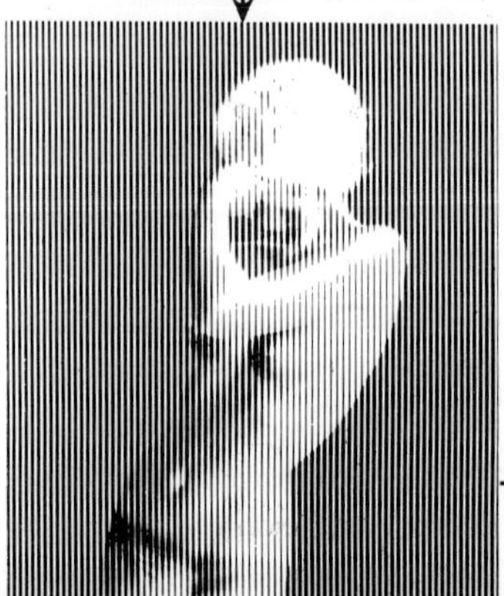

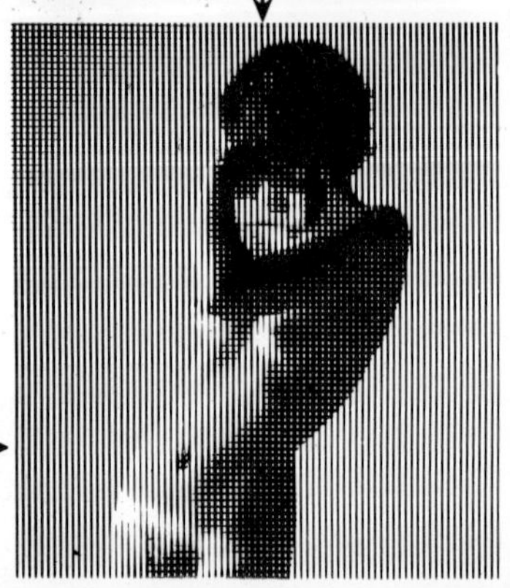

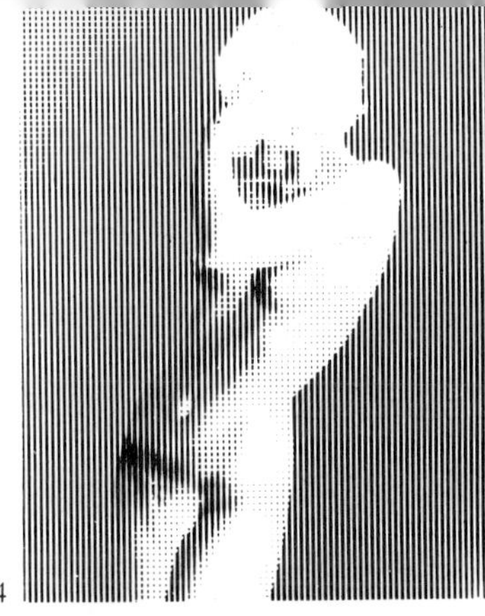

4

it was perforated for registration later.

Stage Two: Both diapositives are separately copied on to 081p film so as to produce a pair of negatives in which the half-tones are reduced.

Stage Three: Expose (a) and (b) negatives successively on to the same piece of film.

Stage Four: Make a negative of the third stage and from this you can produce positive paper prints.

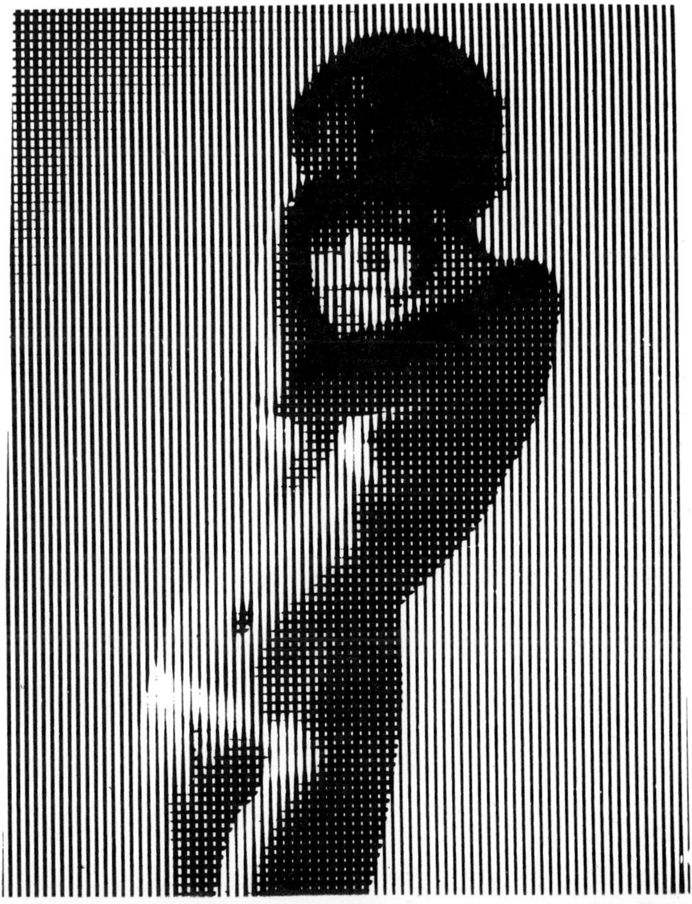

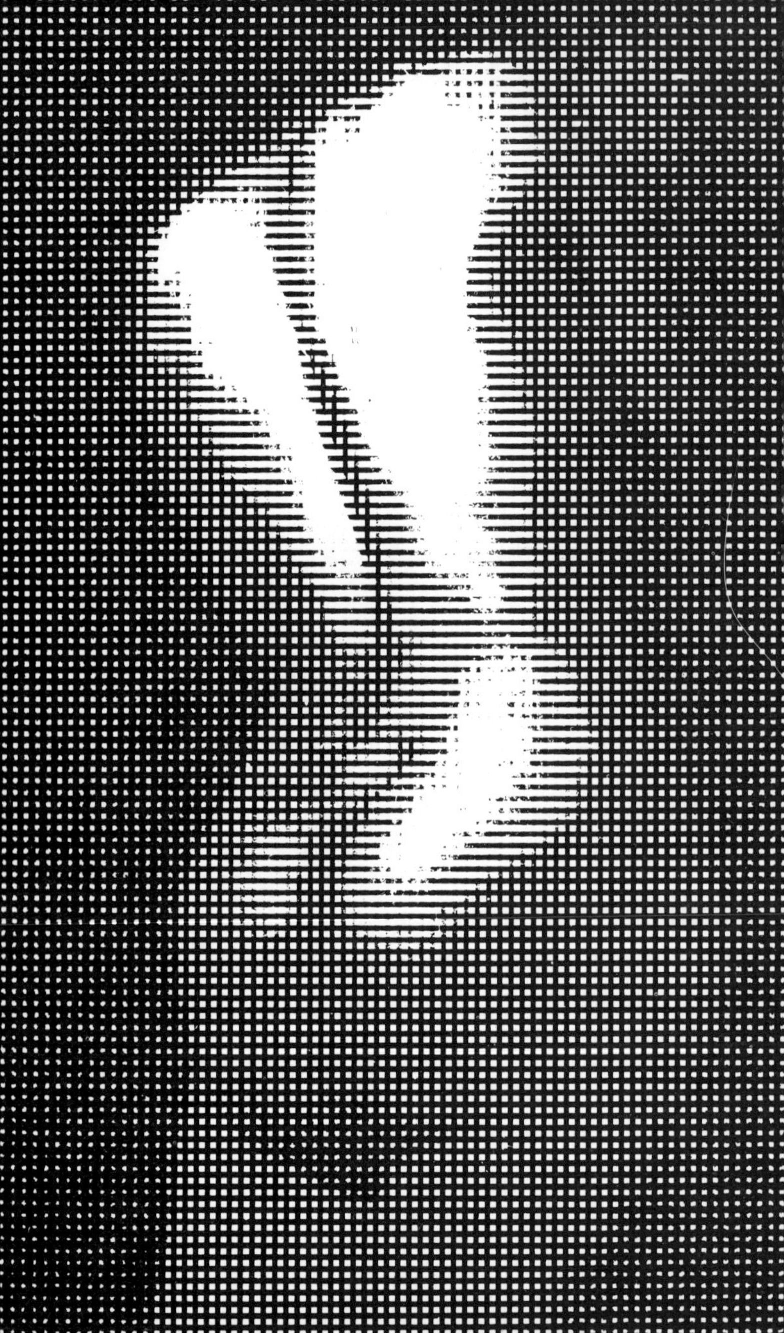

Appendix

In this appendix, I am going to go in more detail into some of the technical matters mentioned in this book. So, if you have plenty of experience of this sort of thing already, you will probably decide to give this section a miss. On the other hand, since it also gives more detailed descriptions of some of the techniques described elsewhere in this book, it might still be worth a look.

A word on equipment . . .

The first word on equipment is that you don't need any. That is to say, you don't need anything special. All you need is ordinary photographic equipment and one or two odd items that you can put together yourself.

Of course, you need a camera. Miniature format will do, but if you can lay your hands on anything larger (say 9 × 12 cm or 3¼ × 4¼ in), then so much the better. If you are using a miniature camera a 6 × 9 cm (2½ × 3½ in) enlarger will be needed, this being the combination most often encountered in this work. The miniature negatives can, without a lot of trouble (certainly if you use intermediate negatives), be blown up to 6 × 9 cm.

This size is much easier to work with. You may be able to put 35 mm negs in register but the accuracy and therefore the time involved will be that much greater. Also, registering the negatives by red light is still more difficult.

If you don't have a 6× 9 cm enlarger and haven't the patience for very painstaking work, then you can work in 9 × 12 cm. Simply follow the procedures as described until you come to the final diapositive. Then put it on a lightbox and load your miniature camera with document reproduction film. If you then photograph it, you will end up with a pin-sharp negative from which to make your prints using your own enlarger.

We have mentioned the enlarger several times and it should be apparent that such an essential item of equipment will have to be of the highest possible quality. Such points as the parallelism of negative carrier and baseboard are vital to the success of many of the processes described above. With screens, for example, the pattern will be distorted if there is the least deviation from the parallel. Also, the lens must be able to project a sharp image right up to the corners of the format with which you are working. The focusing controls grain size on hard paper and it must be the san e size throughout the print, otherwise it will look odd when you enlarge it up to the point where the grain becomes visible. Another useful thing to find out about your enlarger is at what aperture the lens has its maximum sharpness. Not all lenses project their sharpest images at the smallest available aperture. We have also mentioned lightboxes. For preference, choose one with a fluorescent (cold) light source. Pieces of film often have to be left on the lightbox for quite some time and they will curl up unless they can be kept cool.

For printing, an ordinary printing frame will do very nicely. There are other ways – a printing box, for instance – but a frame is almost indispensable. An old fashioned half plate frame will do nicely.

Although it is not essential an electric fan will come in very handy for all the intermediate prints you will have to dry. Some of the procedures described so briefly above can be very time-consuming and anything that helps to reduce that time will be welcome.

Finally, it is virtually impossible to work without a good darkroom timer and the more accurate it is, the better. For preference, it should be accurate to half a second and you should be able to read it easily by red light.

After that, all you need are a couple of extra dishes and a large and a small retouching brush. There are one or two things we have mentioned here and there that you can make yourself but they can be knocked up in half an hour or so without a lot of difficulty.

. . . and another word on method

Always keep a notebook handy and write down everything you do. Put down the negative numbers in every case and note the magnifications used, the materials, the developer and its dilution; and especially the temperature. You will find that you have to control the temperature as carefully as you do with colour so keep it constant at all times.

Making an accurate record brings a number of advantages. In the first place, you will get consistent results because you know exactly what you are doing. Second, if you do obtain an interesting result, you can see exactly why you got it and will be able to get it again. In this way, you will develop your personal photographic style.

Finally, so far as method is concerned, you have to decide whether or not the method has worked for you. The techniques you have available enable you to shape the image the way you want it, so go ahead and do it. Take no notice of what anyone else might say, no matter how many letters he has after his name. But I digress: I should keep to technique. Not that there is much left to say now except that I hope you manage to keep it as it should be – a medium for expressing your own feelings and not as an end in itself

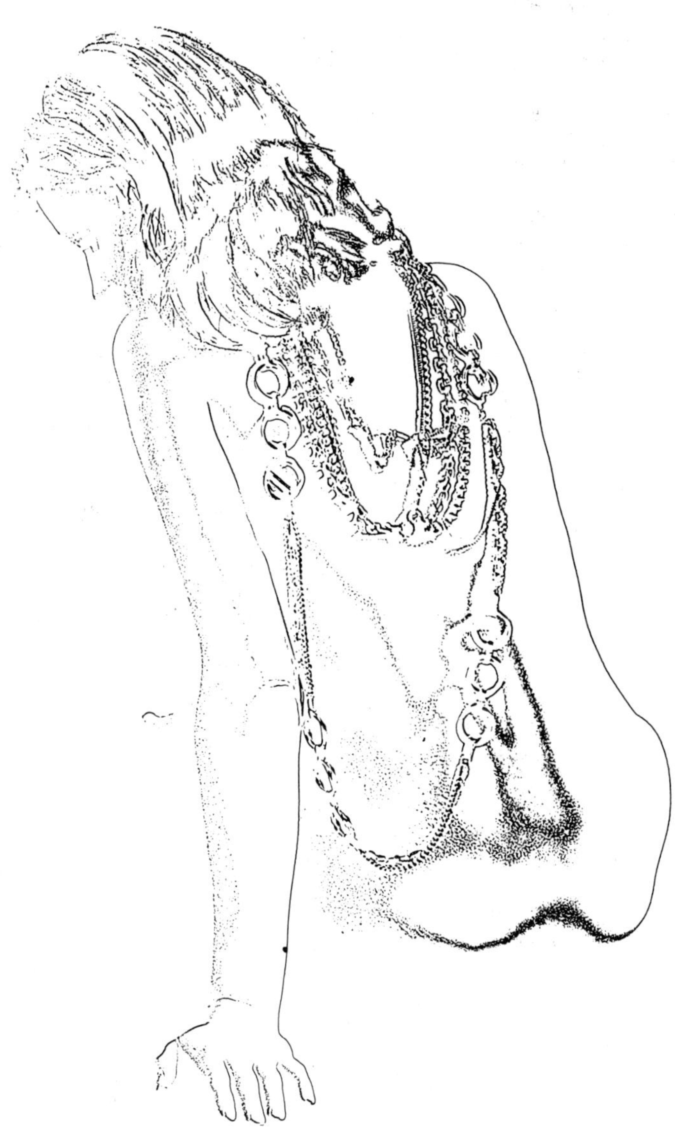

Graphic material

There are one or two difficulties concerned with graphic materials with which I should like to deal here. Let's deal with them under headings.

Material: By and large, you will need two basic types of film material – a normal half-tone film, and a hard material of a fairly extreme type. Most manufacturers produce these materials and the techniques will work with the materials of any reputable manufacturer.
The Agfa codings are as follows: For half-tone film, N31p or N33p. These codes have a meaning and are built up quite logically. The first letter refers to the colour sensitivity of the film. The letter N means "non-ortho", i.e. insensitive to red light; O means orthochromatic and P means panchromatic. Then there is a two-figure number which refers to the hardness grade. The softest film is coded 20, and the hardest 80. The second digit of this two-figure code indicates the thickness of the support. The small letter p at the end of the code number means that the film has a polyester base and so should not be stretched or crimped during processing.
The Kodak equivalent of the half tone film is Commercial Ortho film on an Estar base. A film much referred to in this book and having virtually no half-tones is Agfa O81p, which is equivalent to Kodak's Kodalith Ortho film Type 3 Estar. Agfa-Gevaert also market N81p which, as you can see, is not colour sensitive at all and can therefore be used with a yellow-green safelight. This has the added advantage for the relatively inexperienced operator that the image can be seen as it develops and it can be set up in register more easily.

Format: For some inscrutable reason these graphic materials are not available in amateur packs. The smallest format available is 9 × 12 cm (3¼ × 4¼ in). You can cut this to size with scissors but cutting with a knife is both quicker and more accurate. The best way to tackle this is to cut a groove into a baseboard at the appropriate distance from the edge and exactly parallel to it. The film is laid on the board, and then a razor-sharp knife is slid along the groove, cutting the film neatly and precisely to size. It is essential to keep the knife as sharp as possible, especially with polyester bases which can be very tough. If you have a print trimmer it is easy to fix guides which will enable very accurate cuts to be made.

Developer: You can use an ordinary paper developer which is nowadays available in fluid form under the trade name of Johnsons Universal. You can, of course, use other types of paper developer or even mix a developer for yourself but I would not recommend the latter course. In the first place, you will find it rather difficult to weigh out precise quantities of materials. This means that the solutions you mix will probably not be consistent and the results they give will be unpredictable. The manufacturers of developers go to a great deal of time and trouble and invest huge quantities of money in equipment just to ensure a constant quality, so it seems quite ridiculous to compete with him. In any case haven't you got better things to do with your time than mix chemicals?

Development: Once, on one of my courses, when I lifted a film out of the developer with tongs someone asked me "Do you do that to impress us?". Well, the answer was "no", because I always do it whether in front of a class of students or alone in my own darkroom. I believe in using pure chemicals and in keeping them pure; using tongs is one of the ways of guaranteeing purity.
Another reason, of course, is that you might be allergic to one or other of the chemicals used – metol is perhaps the greatest villain in this respect. And don't say that you aren't sensitive to these things: allergies can build up over the years and erupt suddenly; then the darkroom becomes a nightmare place to work in. You may find it hard to believe, but there have been cases of photographers who quite happily splashed about in developer for years with no ill effect but now get a skin reaction if they so much as go near a darkroom. So always use tongs or rubber gloves. Gloves give better protection to the skin although they are unfortunately not so practical.
Once the film is in the developer you have to keep it moving. You also have to keep the temperature constant. It doesn't n uch matter what the temperature is as long as it lies between 18°C and 24°C, and is kept constant throughout the developing time. The best time for most papers is about 2 min. at 20°C; a longer time will give a harder result and a shorter time a softer result.

Fixing and washing: Because of the larger number of intermediate stages in these processes, the shortest possible fixing and washing times are advisable. As it happens, the fixing time for Agfa O81 is shorter than average because it has a thinner-than-average emulsion. So you should fix until the film is completely clear and you can keep the washing time down to about 3 minutes if you use running water. Film treated in this way will not have a very long life but once it has been used in the intermediate stages it is finished with anyway. Naturally, the final negative should get the full treatment if you want to keep it for any length of time.

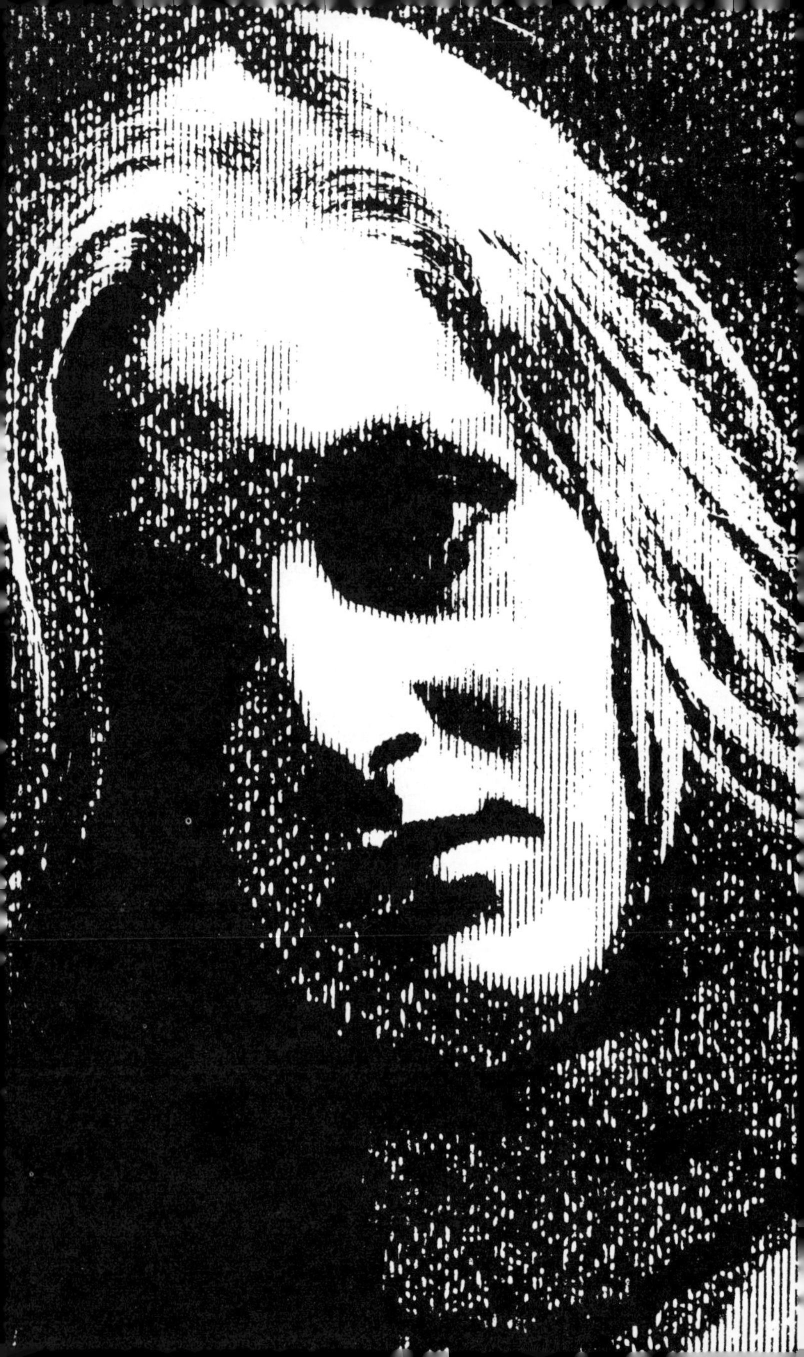

Drying: An electric fan or hairdryer is very useful here. If using O81p film, be very careful not to stretch it or crimp it.

Spotting: On very hard films, spotting-out will often be necessary. No matter how accurately and neatly you work, you will still find minute little spots appearing on the dark parts of your negatives. This is not dust but is in fact a property of the hard emulsion.

You set about getting rid of these little "pinholes" by using a small brush and retouching paint. This paint comes in handy little tubes or pots and can be thinned with water to the required consistency. The consistency is about right when the paint dries immediately it leaves the brush. If you have any left over when you have finished there is no need to throw it away. It can be dissolved in water again but you must make sure it is all dissolved.

The actual spotting-out can best be done on the back of the film. The advantage of this is that if you do make a mistake and go over a line you can wipe away the paint with a damp cloth. On the emulsion side it would all have to be washed off, and sometimes the emulsion could be damaged. Don't use too much paint, otherwise it will stay tacky for a long time.

You can also use this paint for blocking in whole areas of the image, if need be. The sort of thing I mean is the technique used in platemaking for blocking out unwanted backgrounds. You simply paint out the whole background and leave the figure standing against a plain colour. The one thing needed here is a very delicate touch along the outlines of the figure.

Retouching with chemicals: The process described above is what you might call mechanical retouching; a similar effect can be achieved with the use of chemicals.

You normally start with a soft diapositive and when a negative is made from this on to O81 or similar, some of the detail may be lost because the diapositive is too dark. Reduction, as the process is called, is often the answer.

First, the film is well soaked in water and then lightly wiped with a clean leather or with wiping tongs. Next it is laid on a *watertight* lightbox and you can start work. For safety's sake it is essential that no water can leak on to the lamps or holders.

Farmer's Reducer gives best results. You should work with two brushes, one for the reducer and the other for water to dilute it. All the books will tell you that these brushes should not be bound with metal but they won't tell you where to get such brushes. The area to be reduced is now painted with solution and you have to have a deft hand with the water brush and a good eye to keep it where you want it as well as to blend it in. Once you have achieved the effect you want, wash the film with water until all trace of yellow stain disappears. The process can be repeated as often as necessary.

You can make up Farmer solution yourself and the proportions are not too critical. There are two solutions; Solution A consisting of 50g of potassium ferricyanide dissolved in 1000ml of water, and Solution B made up of 200g of sodium thiosulphate (hypo) in 1000ml of water. To use the solutions, equal parts of A and B should be mixed and for general use the mixture should be diluted with eight parts of water. However, for a first attempt you could dilute it with 12 parts of water to get a slower reaction.

In the former concentration, the highlights will bleach out fairly quickly and the half-tones later, but it will be quite a while before the darkest areas will be affected. This reducer is not suitable for overall reduction of the in age.

The proportions of A and B in the mixture have an effect on the result. The more of A there is, the more the reducing effect acts on the half-tones.

It is probably best to try this out on an ordinary print and see what results you get before working on an important negative or print.

Intensification: There can be times when longer exposures produce too heavy an image and loss of detail. In such cases it is often advisable to go for a shorter exposure and a longer development time, and then to use a chemical technique to intensify the image. This is done quite simply by using an intensifier based on mercury iodide such as that produced by Tetenal.

Methods of registering: It is often necessary to bring two or more images precisely into register and there can be some difficulty in achieving this. The simplest method is to copy the final negative on to positives and then to superimpose them as accurately as possible. When they are exactly right, stick them together with a piece of adhesive tape.

Unfortunately, this not as simple as it sounds: it's one of those jobs where you need three hands! So you have to print one of the diapositives on a larger piece of material than the other. Then, cut two pieces of adhesive tape to size and stick them on to the back of your left index finger. When you get the two diapositives accurately in place, hold them there with your thumbs and middle fingers and fiddle one of the pieces of tape off the back of your finger using the right index finger; then lay it carefully down to hold the film in place. The worst is now over and all you have to do is to repeat the manoeuvre with the other

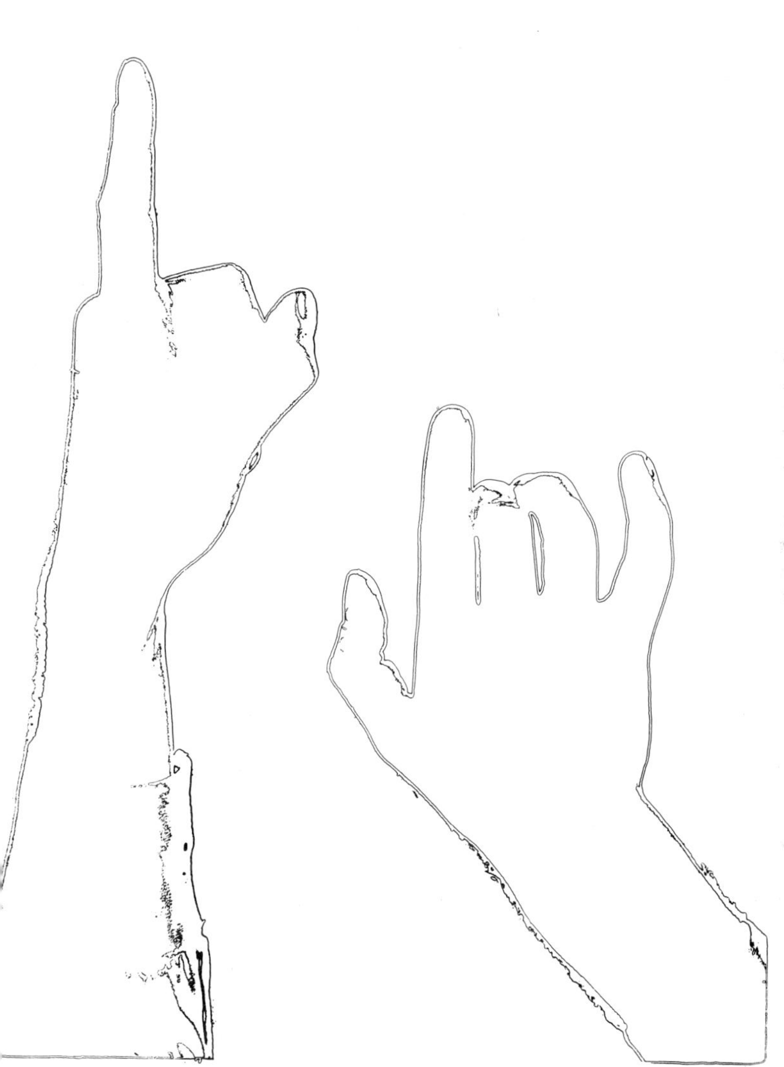

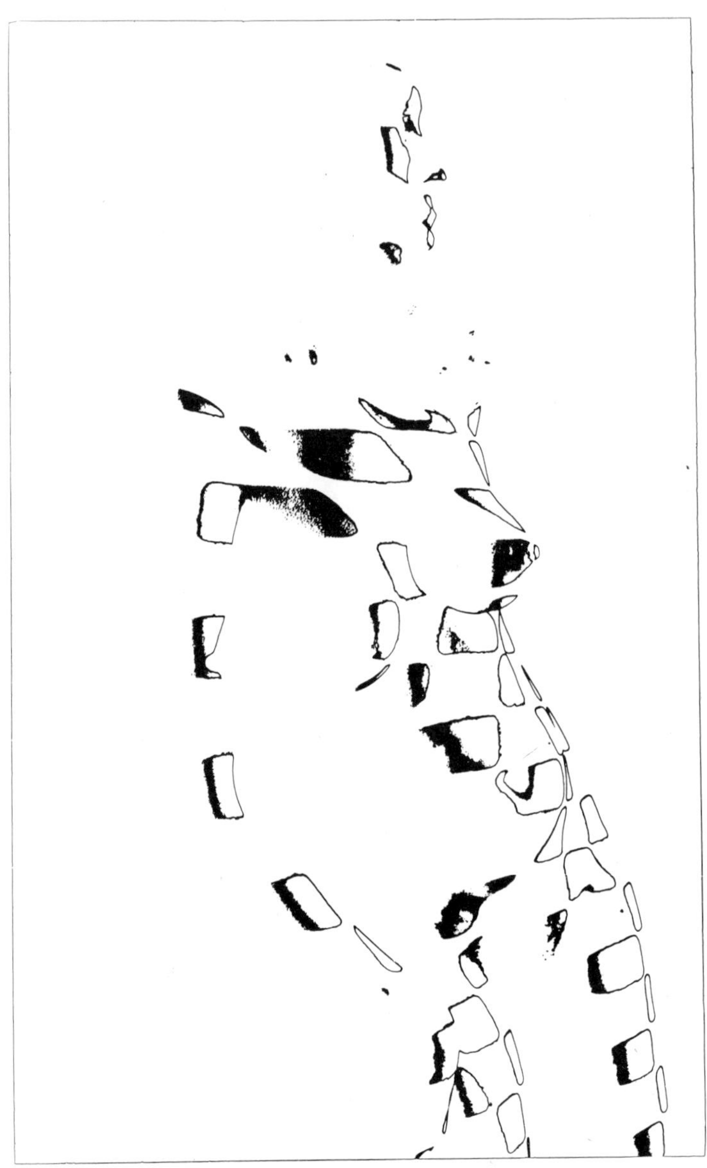

piece of tape so that both diapositives are firmly located. You can then proceed to stick them together at your leisure.

This method is useful only when the diapositives have two clear points that can be used as locators – points such as highlights in the eye, or a mole, or some other sharply-defined but tiny feature. Such features should be as far apart as possible in order to get the greatest accuracy. If there are no features like this or if they are obliterated by the use of screens, you will have to put registration marks at the edges of the print.

These can be bought in the form of little crosses on adhesive film which are stuck on to the first negative. They will appear on each copy you make afterwards thus making it very easy to get copies into register. The only difficulty that can arise is when parallax occurs, as when the two copies are held at some distance apart as for example in the tone-line process. Here it is very difficult to get the eye right above the workpiece and errors in register can easily occur. Even in the smaller formats it is still difficult and a great deal of care and patience may be required to get things exactly right.

Best of all, of course, is a perforator system. You can get extremely accurate perforators with very sophisticated register apparatus but, naturally, you have to pay for this sort of luxury.

However, such accuracy is more than you really need in photographics, and in fact you can get away with a good office punch. You will still need two needles or rods to hold the film in place, and they will have to be the exact diameter of the punched holes. Unfortunately, you are unlikely to find a pair of these of just the right size lying at the back of your odds and ends drawer, so you might like to consider another system.

This is called Passösen and it is manufactured by Agfa. Quite likely, your dealer may not have heard of it because it is handled by the graphic materials division which is a separate entity.

With this system, the material is perforated and then the studs are pressed through it a good distance apart. The studs are then stuck to a small board with glue and a clear glass plate of the same size as the board is held in place with two bulldog clips on each side to keep everything in place. Once you've worked with this system for a while, you'll find you can't do without it.

Faults with pseudo-solarisation

There are four variable factors involved in this technique and any one of them can go wrong. It is perhaps as well to identify them so that faults can be put right with as little frustration as possible.

If your first attempt doesn't go right – and this is very often the case – it will be due to one of these four factors. Therefore you must alter them one at a time until you find which one was responsible for your failure. If you don't work systematically, however, you will be relying on guesswork and this will only take more time in the long run.

The first exposure: This should not be too long. There must be white areas left in the film or the secondary exposure will have no effect. On the other hand, this first exposure must not be too short. In other words, it is essential to get just the right density with this first exposure. An indication of the correct exposure is the time in which the image appears. It should begin to appear not more than ten seconds after being immersed in a paper developer. If the exposure was too short no lines will be visible. Also, too short a first exposure will show up as a grey image and a complete blackening after the secondary exposure.

The first development: If this is too long, you will also get a completely black film. If, on the other hand, it is too short the result will be a low-contrast positive if a positive was used at the start. It is a bit like a solarization in which the image is completely reversed.

The second exposure: Here, too long an exposure time results in a completely black film. Too short an exposure will give you a grey negative.

The second development: Too long a time in the developer is easily recognized by the close-running solarization lines. Although it is best to experiment until you get things exactly right, you can sometimes make another print on to film that will produce a better result when it is eventually printed out on to paper. It can often be improved by treating the whole film in Farmer's reducer.
If the development time is too short, the parts affected by the second exposure are usually pale and somewhat spotty. The line can be seen, but won't print.
In general, you mustn't take this development right through to full density. A couple of trial prints will soon show you just how far along that road you have to go to get the best possible result.

Working with Agfacontour film

Unfortunately, I haven't the space here to give you a full description of Agfacontour, and so I will have to confine myself to giving you just a few tips to help you. If you want the full picture, you should obtain a copy of *Agfacontour-Professional and Photographics*, which is published by Agfa-Gevaert. It will answer all your questions.
The first thing you have to understand about this film is that it has been

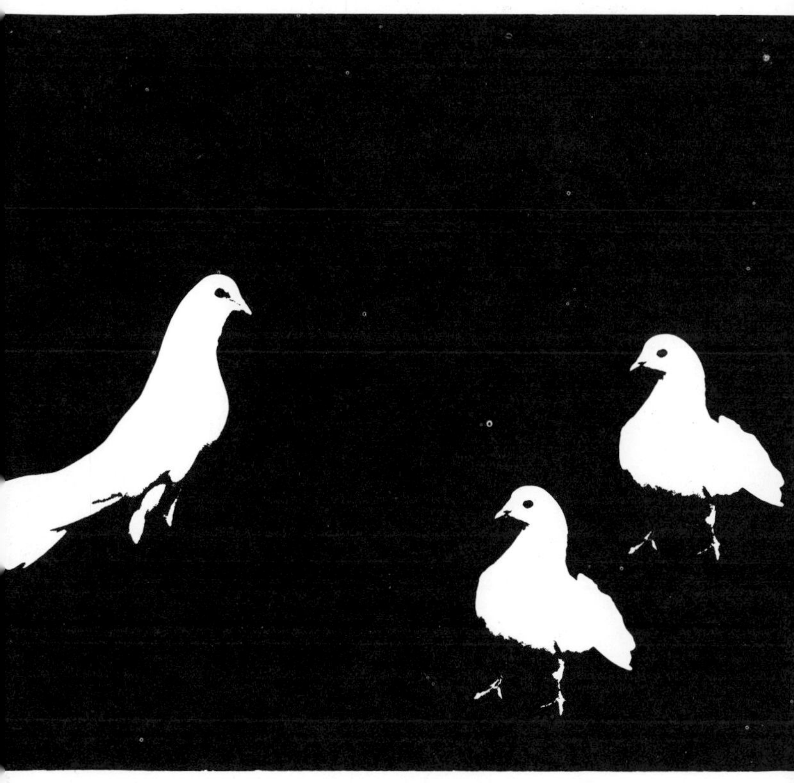

designed to produce both a positive and a negative image simultaneously. The fact that it sometimes produces either a positive or a negative image only means that the other half of the total image – the complementary positive or negative – has been pushed over the edge of the tone-scale.

Agfacontour is intended primarily for scientific and technical use. If you have a step wedge and a densitometer there is no problem, but otherwise trial and error is the only way. All you can do is make a series of successive approximations. In their instructions Agfa mention an exposure of 5 seconds. With my equipment I find that the exposure should be nearer 30 seconds. So you should start by making a set of test exposures at quite large intervals – say, multiplying by four: 2, 8, 32 sec, etc. Then, if necessary, you could make a second series by doubling these, and so come near to the ideal exposure.

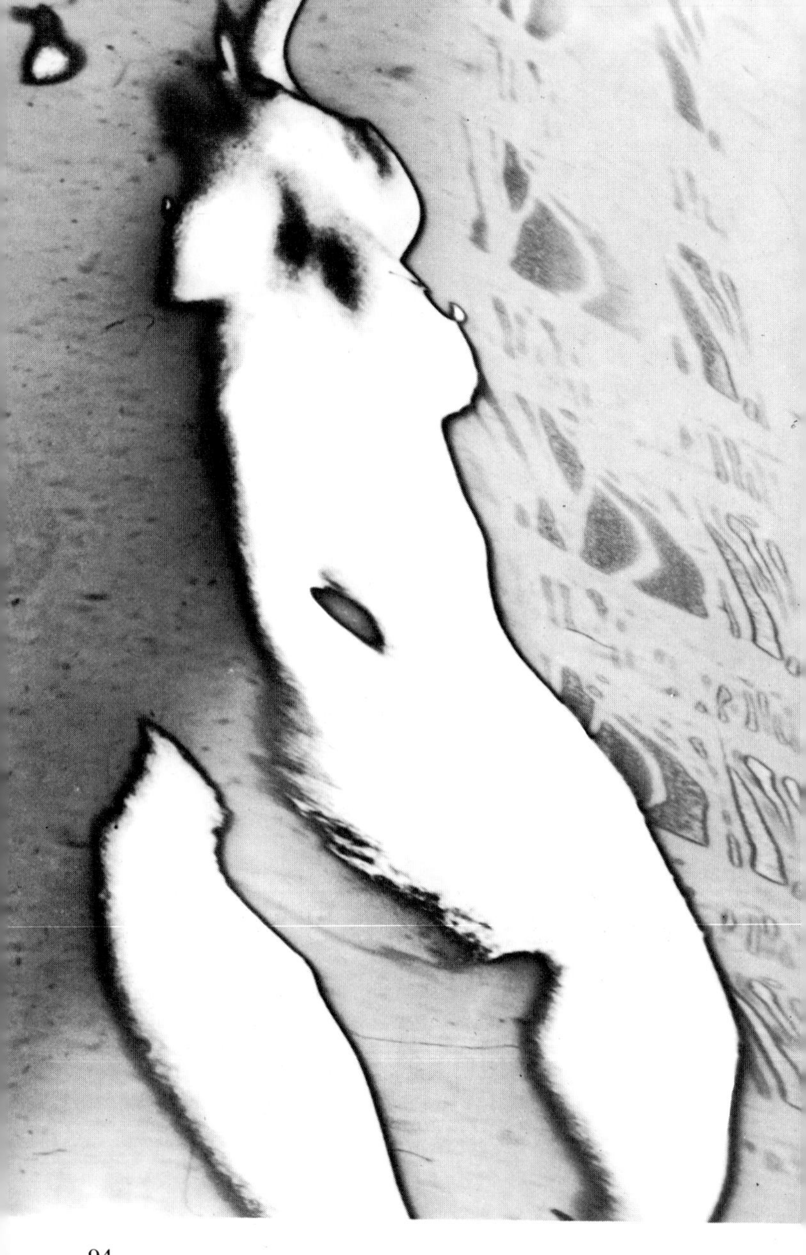

In direct contrast to colour material, a yellow filter slows down Agfacontour. I mention this because I once walked into that trap after I had spent the whole day working with colour material. I had overlooked the fact that ortho-material has roughly half the sensitivity in the blue part of the spectrum.

Development is critical and this of course involves temperature, time, agitation and the degree of exhaustion in the special developer that has to be used. In this respect, I would advise you to use only small quantities of developer and make up a fresh supply regularly.

Finally, the great advantage of this type of film, as opposed to other photographic techniques, is the extent to which the line effect can be controlled by the use of yellow filters.

Colours

It is a very good thing to get a clear idea of where the possibilities and the limits lie, with regard to colour, although the principles are very simple.

When you print a black-and-white negative on to Positive-M film, using a coloured filter, there will be in the print made from the resulting colour negative the same colour as that of the filter. Additive filtering produces more saturated colours than subtractive filtering. With the last filters applied relatively high values are necessary.

So now let us go through the process of making a colour solarization, just to give you a better idea. The first exposure is made with Agfa filters set at 100:–:–, so the result will come out as yellow. Then I give a second exposure in a preponderantly green colour (filters at 300:–:200) to the unexposed background which was black in the diapositive. This produces a colour that, with a little imagination, could be called orange.

Then there's an extra difficulty. Positive-M film is designed to be used with masked negatives; therefore the unmasked materials we use will produce a colour cast. Since the complementary colour of green is now well established, the filters are set at neutral (–:–:–) for the next copy, with magenta (–:200:–) being used for the secondary exposure. Along with the blue already present we get the orange that I'd hoped for. However, we still have to do more copying. The first exposure is therefore made without filters, and the second exposure with filters 300:–:–, that will give a bluish tint to the areas not yet affected. This comes out as a deep bordeaux red in the final print.

Solarisation in colour

Experience gained in black-and-white work is very valuable when making colour solarisations. You don't get lines if the first and second

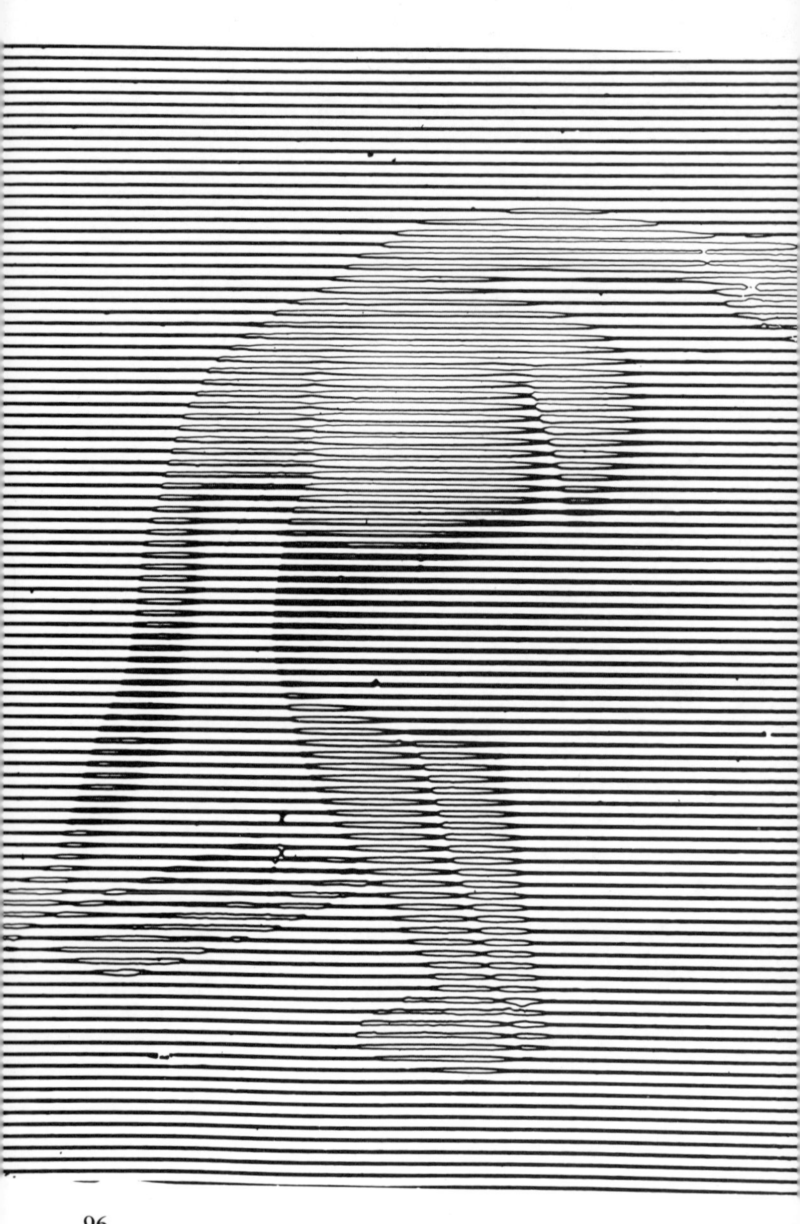

exposures are too short. These are critical and are the main means by which the effect is controlled; development is left to itself–first one, 5 minutes at 24°C, then a good wash, the secondary exposure, a second development of 2 minutes, followed by stopbath, fixer and bleach as usual.

After the first exposure, the piece of film is put into a light-tight box while you remove the negative from the holder, set up the filters for the second exposure and put a dish of clean water in the beam of the enlarger. The masking negative is then put into the enlarger and adjusted so that the surface of the water is precisely illuminated with no reflections coming from the walls of the dish because these can give unwanted patterns to the film.

You then begin the development and, after washing the film, place it in the dish of clean water. Wait for a few seconds to let the ripples die down on the surface and then give the second exposure. Any small faults in the colour can be corrected by filtering during the remainder of the processing.